ARCHITECTURE AND URBANISM
2024:03 No.642

発行者
吉田信之

編集長
佐藤綾子

ゲスト・エディター
トム・デポー
アンドリュー・クランシー

編集
アメナ・ラマン
張紫微

レイアウト制作
安藤聡（pickles design）

編集委員
バリー・バーグドール
ジョヴァンナ・ボラーシ

デザイン
マッシモ・ヴィネリ

©建築と都市　642号　令和6年2月27日発行
毎月1回27日発行
定価：2,852円（本体2,593円）
年間購読料34,224円（年12冊／税・送料込み）
発行：株式会社エー・アンド・ユー
〒100-6017　東京都千代田区霞が関三丁目
2番5号霞が関ビルディング17階
電話：（03）6205-4384　FAX：（03）6205-4387
青山ハウス
〒107-0062　東京都港区南青山二丁目19番14号
電話：（03）6455-5597　FAX：（03）6455-5583
E-mail: au@japan-architect.co.jp
URL: https://japan-architect.co.jp
振替：00130-5-98119
印刷：大日本印刷株式会社
取次店＝トーハン・日販・鍬谷・西村・
楽天ブックスネットワーク

特集：
アイルランドの建築
建築家6組による住宅20選

序：
ハウス・フォー・ヒーロー　アイルランドの新しい建築　4
トム・デポー

対談：
すべてのパーツに意味がある　6
トム・デポー、アンドリュー・クランシー

クランシー・ムーア・アーキテクツ

丘の上の家　14

マルグレイヴ　26

アイルズベリー　30

小説家の部屋　36

スティーヴ・ラーキン・アーキテクツ

バリーブレイクの家　42

ボグウェストの家　52

スライガフの家　58

ライアン・W・ケニハン・アーキテクツ

ドロムリー・ハウス　72

バルトラスナ・ハウス　78

ミドル・ハウス　86

ビーチ・ロード・ハウス　90

TAKAアーキテクツ

ミドルトン・パーク・ゲート・ロッジ　102

ハウス4　112

ブライトン・ロード　116

ルーベン・ストリート　122

デイヴィッド・リーチ・アーキテクツ

家と庭　128

温室　136

tobアーキテクト

キラン・ファームハウス　144

ルーベン・ストリート　152

ザ・キー　156

表紙：トム・デポー「ダイサート」。
裏表紙：クランシー・ムーア・アーキテクツ「マルグレイヴ」。

ARCHITECTURE AND URBANISM
2024:03   No.642

Publisher:
Nobuyuki Yoshida

Editor in Chief:
Ayako Sato

Guest Editors:
Tom de Paor
Andrew Clancy

Editor:
Amena Rahman
Zhang Ziwei

Layout:
Satoshi Ando (pickles design)

Copyeditor:
Amy Teschner

Editorial Board:
Barry Bergdoll
Giovanna Borasi

Design:
Massimo Vignelli

Distributor:
Shinkenchiku-sha Co., Ltd.

© 2024 A+U Publishing Co., Ltd.
Printed in Japan
Published by A+U Publishing Co., Ltd.
Kasumigaseki Building 17F, 3-2-5,
Kasumigaseki, Chiyoda-ku, Tokyo
100-6017, Japan
Tel: +81-3-6205-4384   Fax: +81-3-6205-4387
Aoyama House
2-19-14 Minamiaoyama, Minato-ku, Tokyo
107-0062, Japan
Tel: +81-3-6455-5597   Fax: +81-3-6455-5583
Email: au@japan-architect.co.jp
URL: https://au-magazine.com

ISBN 978-4-9002-1301-2
a+u = Architecture and Urbanism is handled
exclusively
by Shinkenchiku-sha Co., Ltd.:
Kasumigaseki Building 17F, 3-2-5,
Kasumigaseki, Chiyoda-ku, Tokyo
100-6017, Japan
Tel: +81-3-6205-4380   Fax: +81-3-6205-4386
Email: ja-business@japan-architect.co.jp
Subscription rate for 2024 outside Japan
¥42,000 (Airmail – China, South Korea,
Taiwan), ¥43,000 (Airmail – Asia not including
China, South Korea, Taiwan), ¥49,000 (Airmail
– Oceania, Canada, Mexico, Middle East,
Europe), ¥55,000 (Airmail – United States,
Central and South America (not including
Mexico), Africa).
US Dollars, Euro, and Sterling Pounds
equivalent to the above Japanese Yen prices
are acceptable. When you remit, please convert
to the current exchange rate.

Feature:
Irish Architecture
20 Houses by 6 Architects

Introduction:
House for hero – New Irish Architecture   4
Tom de Paor

Conversation:
No Small Parts   6
Tom de Paor and Andrew Clancy

Clancy Moore Architects

House on a Hill   14

Mulgrave   26

Ailesbury   30

Writers Room   36

Steve Larkin Architects

House at Ballyblake   42

House at Bogwest   52

House at Slyguff   58

Ryan W. Kennihan Architects

Dromlee House   72

Baltrasna House   78

Middle House   86

Beach Road House   90

TAKA architects

Middleton Park Gate Lodge   102

House 4   112

Brighton Road   116

Reuben Street   122

David Leech Architects

House and a Garden   128

Conservatory Room   136

t o b Architect

Killan Farmhouse   144

Reuben Street   152

The Quay   156

Front cover: Tom de Paor, Dysart. Photo by Peter Maybury.
Back cover: Clancy Moore Architects, Mulgrave. Photo courtesy of the architect.

Feature:
Irish Architecture
20 Houses by 6 Architects

特集：
アイルランドの建築
建築家6組による住宅20選

a+u's March issue presents Irish architecture through 20 houses by 6 architecture firms. These houses, nestled in the landscape of Ireland, paint a portrait of the physical conditions of the island. Architects Tom de Paor and Andrew Clancy serve as guest editors and begin the feature in conversation. They describe Ireland as being gently exhausted and without past glories, but not yet melancholic. The 20 houses responding to the island are practically designed yet with sensitive qualities of "dry and wet," "soft lighting and fleeting shadows," and "modeling and its staining." These houses are individual attempts by their architects to find something that was already "constructed, abandoned, found" and to discover their own architectural language in Ireland. Their images, drawings, and give form to a notably new Irish architecture. (*a+u*)

『a+u』3月号では、建築家6組による20の住宅を通して、アイルランドの建築を特集する。アイルランドの地面に建てられたこれら住宅群は、この島の一部として島のきわめて物理的な状況を描きだす。本特集は、建築家のトム・デポーとアンドリュー・クランシーをゲスト・エディターに迎え、両者の対話から始まった。「メランコリーも過去の栄光もなく」「幾度となく姿を変える大地」であると彼らが語るこの島では、乾燥と湿度、柔らかい光とはかない影、造形とその色付けが、住宅の質を浮かび上がらせる。20の住宅は、アイルランドという土地にすでに「つくられ、放棄され、みつけだされ」何かを探し求め、自分自身の言語を見つけだそうとする建築家らの試みである。住宅というかたちをとった個々の試みをここに集めることで、イメージ・ドローイング・テキストの群として誌面に見えてくるアイルランドの新しい建築を紹介する。 （編）

Introduction:
House for hero – New Irish Architecture

序：
ハウス・フォー・ヒーロー　アイルランドの新しい建築

It was fun to look at this work with Andrew Clancy's wit and insight. We thought it precise if the Irish edition featured work built on the island, rather than from it.

One task of the architect is the development of language, vital to an architecture that communicates. Some manage one in a career, a few 2, rarely 3. No better place to start than the house, the seat of architecture and most complex and simple of projects, for city and landscape.

I did not visit these buildings, which is not important here, perhaps even an advantage when looking through architects' images, drawings, and texts – self-portraits in their best light, postcards really from a made-up place, inclusive and alert in changeable weather.

An exaggeration of course, as design is, and also an understatement – to omit the middle ground to highlight fore and back – which is the promise of this work, the wish you were here at the heart of architecture.

Tom de Paor
February 6, 2024, Dysart, Ireland

アンドリュー・クランシーと一緒になって、彼のウィットと知識を添えて、この仕事にとり掛かった。この国から発信された作品を載せるのではなく、この島に建てられた作品を掲載すること。アイルランドを特集するこの号ではそれが的を射ていると、二人とも思っている。

建築家に課せられた仕事とは、言語をつくりだすことである。ものを伝える建築には不可欠なことだ。生涯を通して一つ言語をつくることに成功する建築家もいる。二つめに到達する建築家さえいる。三言語こなす人はほとんどいない。その仕事にとり掛かる上で、始めるべきは住宅だ。それは、都市にあっても、自然にあっても、建築の据わる場所であり、いちばん複雑で、いちばんシンプルなプロジェクトである。

私自身はここに載せた住宅を訪ねてはいない。それは問題ではなく、むしろ、建築家たちのイメージ、ドローイング、テキストに目を通す際にはおそらく利点でさえある。これらは彼らの自画像であり、でっちあげの場所からきた絵葉書であり、変わりやすい天候における包容と警戒心である。

もちろん、デザインがそうであるように、前と後ろを際立たせるために中間を省くことは誇張であり、控えめな表現である。それこそがこの仕事の約束であり、ここが建築の中心であってほしいという願いである。

トム・デポー
ダイサート、2024年2月6日

Guest Editors:

Tom de Paor graduated from University College Dublin in 1991, when he commenced practice. An elected fellow of the Royal Institute of Architects of Ireland, international fellow of the Royal Institute of British Architects, and member of Aosdána, he lives and works at Dysart in Wicklow, Ireland. He often collaborates with Peter Maybury under the imprint Gall.

Andrew Clancy is a professor of architecture at Kingston School of Art and directs REGISTER – a research group that encompasses a wide range of means to engage with, research and disseminate thinking about the built environment. He is a visiting professor at Accademia di Architettura Mendrisio and was a visiting professor at Arkitektskolen Aarhus, Denmark, in 2015. He has a PhD from RMIT University and is a member of the Royal Institute of Architects of Ireland.

ゲスト・エディター：

トム・デポーは1991年にユニバーシティ・カレッジ・ダブリンを卒業。アイルランド王立建築家協会フェロー、英国王立建築家協会国際フェロー、アオスダーナ会員。Gall社のもと写真家のピーター・メイベリーとの協働が多くある。

アンドリュー・クランシーは、キングストン美術学校の建築学科教授およびREGISTER（構築環境の研究と普及のための研究グループ）を率いている。メンドリジオ建築アカデミーの客員教授であり、2015年にはデンマークのオーフス建築学校の客員教授を務める。RMIT大学で博士号を取得し、アイルランド王立建築家協会会員。

Conversation:
No Small Parts
Tom de Paor and Andrew Clancy

対談：
すべてのパーツに意味がある
トム・デポー、アンドリュー・クランシー
中田雅章訳

This page: The Rest, *August 2023, Dysart. Photo by Peter Maybury.*

本頁：ダイサート《ザ・レスト》（2013年8月）。

June 6, 2023, Dysart, Ireland

Tom de Paor (TdP): The history of architecture is in some way a history of the house. Is it the most important project?

Andrew Clancy (AC): It might be the most meaningful. There is the depth of the encounter and the nature of autobiography that gets wrapped up in it. Everything is implicated – the people and the place, the most intimate and involved of briefs with the most fraught of economics, an architecture based on contingency, not certainty. It is not arm's length.

TdP: These are all privileged projects / commissions: a dream becomes a conversation which unravels into a reality, a kind of return to the house, remade, again. Some houses in their anonymity, their lack of expression, matter-of-fact function, reasonable aspect from nondescript rooms, offer a freedom that the specifics of the bespoke deny. The clarity won in the organization of dwelling removes as much as it offers, maybe more: its compromise somehow is its beauty. Is the dream house bound to fail?

AC: An interesting question. Conversations only advance here when they get practical, and this is a way into a real depth of encounter. The idealized role of architecture and lifestyle doesn't get set aside – the negotiation of tangible things inevitably navigates there, and then at some point it is captured by an emergent quality – let's call it architecture – which shapes the description anew. The task is to find it again in this new perspective – one no less grounded or idealistic. Preconceptions are unpicked, from both sides, so the house has this compelling capacity to be a fountain of knowledge for architecture, because it's always capturing society in its essential components, more than any other type.

TdP: A self-portrait, and if so, what do these houses say? The avant-garde seems absent here.

AC: You are never asked for something heroic. No one, or very few, wish to live in the fancy house on the hill.

TdP: In the glass house, I am self-conscious . . .

AC: That's the point. You'd have to be comfortable with that feeling. All the time.

TdP: Even in the bathroom. So, the provocation of another way of life is not the question.

2023年6月6日、アイルランド、ダイサートにて

トム・デポー（TdP）：建築の歴史は、住宅の歴史でもあります。それこそいちばん大切な仕事だと思いませんか？

アンドリュー・クランシー（AC）：いちばん意味深いというべきかもしれません。住宅は、人との交わりと自叙伝を刻んでいくものです。すべてがかかわります。人と場所、最も私的かつ経済的に危うさのある側面に触れるものであり、確実性ではなく不確実性にもとづく建築です。住宅には、距離を置いてかかわることはできません。

TdP：例外なく、特別なプロジェクトで、特別な依頼です。夢が対話になり、対話は解きほぐされ現実になります。あたかも住宅に立ち戻って、またもつくり直すかのように。名もなきものであること、自己主張をしないこと、当たり前の機能やごく普通の部屋の合理性、これらの性質をもつことで、つくり込まれたオーダーメイドにはない自由さを獲得する住宅があります。その構成に実現された明確さは、住宅にもたらすのと同じくらい、あるいはそれ以上に、住宅から奪います。妥協こそが住宅の美だと言えないでしょうか？　夢の住宅は、必ず失敗する運命なのでしょうか。

AC：興味深い論点です。対話は、人が現実的になった時にのみ前進します。そして人の交わりの真の深みへの道筋です。建築とライフスタイルの理想的役割が排除されるわけではありません。具体的な物事についての話し合いが否応なく道筋を導き、ある時点でそれは浮かび上がってくる質——これを建築と呼びます——にとらえられます。この質こそが対話に新しいかたちをもたらします。成すべきは、この新たな視点のもと改めて対話——同じくらい地に足がついていて、同じくらい理想を語る対話——を見出すことです。先入観はいずれの側からも解かれています。こうして住宅は説得力のある、建築知識の根源となります。ほかのどの形式と比べても、住宅は常に、自身を構成する不可欠な要素として社会をとらえるからです。

TdP：自画像、だとすると、住宅は何を語るのでしょう？　前衛性は不在であるように思えます。

AC：大胆なもの、ヒーローであることは求められていないでしょう。丘の上の奇抜な家に住みたいと思う人はほとんどいません。

TdP：ガラスの家では人目が気になって……

AC：その通りです。その状態で、常に落ち着いて過ごせなければ無理です。

AC: But the way of life is reestablished in each building. Each of these houses is quietly radical in their own way – reinventing how someone lives in the landscape might happen on the side of thinking about a window. Here we resist saying anything too declarative. And yet the ambition exists, no less clear for that. If there was an Irish space program, we wouldn't say we were going to the moon.

TdP: Yes, not building a spaceship, rather a heat pump.

AC: The heroic impulse speaks to clarities. Of course, these architects use type, abstraction, allusion, and all the rest, but to start not end. Architecture can't come from philosophy or geometry alone but from a rational understanding of the human animal. Its mess and its caprice. Its visceral connection and abstracted dreaming. It is about the parts made seen and unseen, and their making. That's the magic.

TdP: I see a slang here, some kind of vernacular – for instance through the windows, and how they're made, and by who, presumably from up the road.

AC: I think that you can divide the world of architecture into territories where it is still possible to design a window – I mean its frame, its profiles, everything – and make it, and where it is not possible any longer – where it is all system. This architecture is not possible to imagine without a craft tradition; it's common knowledge and relationships – often it's the most cost-effective way to go.

TdP: Practically every window in this place, I don't know if I am ashamed to say, differs – variations on a theme because of the nature of the problems given by the found object. The firm who made them has also made for you and Colm [Moore], but in your case the one-off window manufacturer assembles a curtain wall as he can, by changing his jig. A bespoke thing becomes a system, which gives tension. The conceit of inevitability is not used here.

AC: In any part of a building there is an opportunity to find the powerful idea.

TdP: It is also a tactic of procurement.

AC: So, you can find the radical insight through its parts, the epic in the highly specific. Those who speak of theoretical themes in generalities are looking through the wrong end of the telescope. From the specific we understand the general.

TdP. It is a little shock sometimes to catch your reflection in the window when the place appears projected. An almost after image.

AC: It's in the water; the population is still barely more than half of what it was 2 centuries ago – that does shape things. It adds a tone. Not melancholy, not at all, but there are no past glories, and the ground here has been gone over, many times. The mountains are worn out; it's a gently exhausted thing.

TdP: There is no wilderness.

AC: There hasn't been for a long time. Ireland is small physically but vast temporally. Everything is constructed, abandoned, found. There's always something; often it is the major part of the work, to look for it.

TdP: Is that why these projects seem suspicious of the idea of the spaceship – the exotic thing made of its own pure thinking, landing?

AC: Maybe. There is none of that mythology of newness – there was someone here long before, always. The land bears the evidence.

TdP: The work is not abstract in that sense; there is no green field condition.

AC: This is an island. Objects are not pure; they have a windward side and a sheltered one. It is felt, this archipelago. When sheltered here, it's actually very clement. Never mind an essay of inside and out; it's too reductive – it is more about dry and wet and to what degree and how to address it.

TdP: The light is dilute somehow, too, in a lovely way. The "magnificent play" doesn't happen. Modeling and its staining replace depth – the sky changeable, between the house and its sudden shadow, a fleeting thing. The mood changes all the time and the architecture with it, or the other way round. Form becomes a game of gradient and surface.

AC: And this might return to an earlier point – that the spaceship is best in sharp light. This architecture seeks more amplification; it is an architecture of exaggeration.

TdP: From the constraint of small asks.

AC: Architecture doesn't need a functional alibi.

TdP: There are no small roles.

AC: No small parts.

TdP: It can be a limitation to be fascinated by a little thing but sometimes a show of strength. The challenge is to make enough space for it to be. And so, there is a prejudicing of the apparatus of the house.

AC: There is a hypocrisy to talk about essential qualities independent of their components. These projects have a sense of themselves, not found in manifesto, but in what makes them. That is where it feels the discovery is, whether tectonic or spatial.

TdP: Can there be then a hierarchy between part and the whole?

AC: There is a form, not fully known; the parts are formed in its ambit. It dampens doubt. The form is an agreement which allows the rest to coalesce. So, there is a hierarchy which all this is pushing against, which then is mediated, and the form, not quite set, will shift to this information coming up against it.

TdP: If the part stands out of the ordinary, do we return to the spaceship?

AC: Ordinary is such a strange word because what is everyday is often odd, exuberant, and strange. So, these do not have

TdP：浴室でも。だとすると、新たな生き方を喚起することが目的ではないわけです。

AC：けれど生き方はそれぞれの建物のなかで改めて成り立っていきます。ひとつひとつの住宅は、それぞれ寡黙な革新さをもっています。窓を検討しているうちに、その場所における生き方が再発明されるなんてことがあるかもしれません。この土地で、私たちは断定的に語ることを避けています。それでも確かに、野心はあるものです。アイルランドの宇宙計画は月を目指しはしません。

TdP：宇宙船よりヒート・ポンプをつくりますね。

AC：大胆さへの欲求、ヒーロー欲求は、明確さを必要とします。もちろんここにあげた建築家たちは、形式、抽象化、隠喩などあらゆる手段を使いますが、それはスタート地点であってゴールではありません。建築が哲学や幾何学のみから生まれでることはありません。人という動物を理性で理解することから生まれるのです。人の混沌と気まぐれ、人の理屈を超えたつながりと抽象的な夢を理解することから。目に見えるパーツと隠されたパーツ、そしてそれらをつくることです。それが魔法なのです。

TdP：誌面からはスラング、方言のようなものがみえてきます。たとえば窓、そのつくり方、すぐ近くから来たであろう、それをつくった人を通して。

AC：建築の世界は2つに分かれていると思います。いまだに窓、窓枠や立面全体を設計しつくることができる領域と、もはやすべてがシステムとなりそれが不可能な領域に。窓をつくることができる建築は、ものづくりの伝統、その共有の知識との関係を抜きに想い描くことはできません。多くの場合それが、最もコスト効率のよい進め方なのです。

TdP：ダイサートでは実際に、すべての窓が異なり（それが恥ずべきことなのかどうかはわかりません）、ある主題のもと変化します。そのヴァリエーションは、目的がもたらす問題の性質によります。ここの窓をつくった会社はアンドリューとコルム・ムーアのためにも窓をつくっています。あなたの場合に、窓メーカーが、そのためだけに治具を替え、可能な範囲でカーテン・ウォールを組み立てていますね。特注のものがシステムになり、システムが緊張をもたらします。必然性という驕りはここにはありません。

AC：建物のどのパーツにも、素晴らしいアイディアにつながる可能性はあります。

TdP：調達の方策でもあります。

AC：だからこそパーツ、きわめて特異な部分部分から、本質に迫る洞察を見出すことができるのです。普遍のなかに理論を語る人は、望遠鏡を反対側から使っています。私たちは個から普遍を知るのです。

TdP：窓に場所が映り込んでいるとき、そこに反射した自分の姿をみるのは、時としてちょっとした驚きです。まるで残像のようです。

AC：この場所は水のなかにあって、人口は2世紀前の1.5倍をようやく超える程度に過ぎません。この事実がものをかたちづくっています。それがトーンを添えています。メランコリーなどまったくなく、過去の栄光もありません。大地は、幾度となく姿を変えています。山々は削られ、それはゆっくり姿を消していく存在です。

TdP：手つかずの土地はないです。

AC：ずっと昔からありません。アイルランドは物理的には小さな存在ですが、時間的には悠久の存在です。あらゆるものがつくられ、放棄され、みつけだされています。常に何かがあり、それを探し求めることが我々の仕事の重要な部分となることもあります。

TdP：だからこそこれらプロジェクトは、地に降りてきた宇宙船——純粋な思考からつくられたみたことない存在——という発想に懐疑的であるようなのありませんか？

AC：そうかも知れません。新しさの神話はありません。ここにはずっと前から誰かがいたのです。大地にはその証が刻まれています。

TdP：その意味で、抽象的な仕事は存在しません。これまで何も建てられてこなかった場所などないのですから。

AC：ここは島です。対象は純粋ではありません。風を受ける側と、風から守られる側があります。群島を肌で感じます。風から守られていれば、実はとても穏やかです。内と外を語ることなどどうでもよく、単純化が過ぎています。乾燥と湿気、そしてその程度、それにどう対処するかが問題です。

TdP：光も、ここではとても好ましく、柔らかいです。「神々しい戯れ」が起こることはありません。造形とその色づけが、奥行きに代わります。空は、住宅とそこににわかに射す影、はかないものの間でうつろいます。雰囲気は絶えず変化し、それとともに建築が変わることもあれば、逆のうつろいもあります。形態は傾きと面の戯れになります。

AC：そしてふたたび、先ほどのポイントに戻るのかも知れません。宇宙船は強い光のなかでこそ、最も素晴らしい姿をみせるものです。この建築はさらなる増幅を求めます。それは誇張の建築です。

TdP：小さな依頼の束縛から。

AC：建築には、機能についてのアリバイは必要ありません。

TdP：意味のない役割はありません。

AC：すべてのパーツに意味があります。

TdP：細かいことに集中すると制約になることもありますが、強さにつながることもあり得ます。そのために十分な空間をつくりだすことが課題です。それゆえ、住宅という装置に偏見が生じることになるのです。

AC：構成要素を語ることなく、本質について語ろうとするのは偽善です。これらプロジェクトには個性があります。それはマニフェストに見出されるのではなく、つくりあげているものに見出されます。発見が可能なのは、構造であれ空間であれ、その部分です。

TdP：部分と全体の間にヒエラルキーは存在し得るでしょうか？

AC：すべてが明らかではない形態があって、部分はその範囲に形成されます。それは疑念をとり去ります。形態は残りの部分を結合可能にするとり決めです。そ

some "whisperer" relationship with the ordinary but use it as a search for a vital presence. The project might be found in one piece, and this can be part of the emerging whole. Or the contraflow happens – the irregularity becomes a beautiful serendipity, rather than contrivance to dream back the project. It feels excited. The diagram – the idea writ large – is in some senses the easiest thing to do and doesn't bring a gift with it. A meaningful relationship with architecture, capital, or lowercase "a," is when it understands the human condition – abstraction and order – but inflected.

TdP: The conversation becomes richer as the protagonist is liberated from the need to understand, allowed to just be. That the made place has a bigger intelligence at work, beyond its author. Alert.

AC: Architecture wants the full body in that sense; it needs the intellect, but also needs to know what it's like to be somewhere and call it. You need both. The methods are a means to that moment of embodied judgment. After all, if the drawing is more interesting than the building, why build it? Dealing with space is a play of balance, ensemble, and its choreography. In the thicket of this, is the self of the building, a kind of consciousness. The cultivation of this is the effort.

TdP: And the basis of tectonics, these meetings, their expression, which ask occasionally of decoration – downpipes say, as jewelry. Opportunities are taken here to tug at the sleeve and show the architect's hand, to display facility across the scales, down to one is to one. That attention to detail amplifies the reading of the building?

AC: Yes, the architecture is always implicating itself into somebody's day-to-day.

TdP: And asking to be a hero?

AC: Small "h."

TdP: [whispers] I am the author of your house.

AC: Think of me when the rain falls . . .

TdP: When the toilet flushes.

こには、すべてに当てはめられるヒエラルキーがあり、次いでそこに調和が図られ、そしてかたちが完全には定まっていない形態は、それに照らして生じてくる情報へと移行していきます。

TdP：部分がもし普通より目立つのならば、宇宙船に戻っていくでしょうか？

AC：普通というのはとても不思議な言葉です。私たちの日常は、往々にしてちぐはぐで、型にはまらない不可解なものだからです。ですから、日常が普通の「黒幕」であることはなく、むしろ日常は普通を、不可欠の存在を探し求めるために利用しています。プロジェクトは一つの部分からできていて、そのプロジェクトは新たに姿を現そうとしている全体の部分であるかもしれません。逆もあり得ます。不規則な動きは、振り返ってプロジェクトを夢描く仕掛けではなく、美しい偶然となります。わくわくしますね。ダイアグラム――拡大表示されたアイディア――はある意味いちばん簡単で、何かをもたらすことはありません。大文字でも小文字でも、建築との意味のある関係は、人のありよう――抽象概念と秩序――を理解したときに生まれますが、それは屈折しています。

TdP：対話は、それを主導する人が理解することから解放され、ありのままであることを許されたときに、豊かなものになります。つくられた場所には、そのつくり手を超えて、より大きな知性が作用するものです。油断してはなりません。

AC：その意味で、建築は身体を必要とします。知性を必要ともしますが、どこかに存在するとはどのようなことかを知り、それを実行することも必要です。両者が必要なのです。方法は、具現化された判断の瞬間へと向かうための手段です。最終的にドローイングが建物より面白いならば、なぜ建てるのでしょうか？ 空間を扱うとは、バランスとアンサンブル、そしてその動きの演出です。この錯綜のうちにあるのが建築の自我、ある種の意識です。これを深めていくのが努力なのです。

TdP：その構造の拠りどころ、こうした対話、時として装飾――たとえば宝飾としての雨樋のような――を求めるそれぞれの表現。ここには、踏み込んで建築家の真の狙いを明らかにする、1対1のスケールに至るまで、さまざまな尺度で機能を示す機会があります。細部への意識は、建築の読みとりを深いものにするでしょうか？

AC：そうですね。建築は常に、建築そのものを誰かの日常に結びつけています。

TdP：そしてヒーローになれと？

AC：小文字のヒーローにね。

TdP：（小声で）私はあなたの家の作者ですよ。

AC：雨の日には私のことを思いだしてください……

TdP：トイレを流すときにね。

1. Clancy Moore Architects, House on a Hill
2. Clancy Moore Architects, Mulgrave
3. Clancy Moore Architects, Ailesbury
4. Clancy Moore Architects, Writers Room
5. Steve Larkin Architects, House at Ballyblake
6. Steve Larkin Architects, House at Bogwest
7. Steve Larkin Architects, House at Slyguff
8. Ryan W. Kennihan Architects, Dromlee House
9. Ryan W. Kennihan Architects, Baltrasna House
10. Ryan W. Kennihan Architects, Middle House
11. Ryan W. Kennihan Architects, Beach Road House
12. TAKA architects, Middleton Park Gate Lodge
13. TAKA architects, House 4
14. TAKA architects, Brighton Road
15. TAKA architects, Reuben Street
16. David Leech Architects, House and a Garden
17. David Leech Architects, Conservatory Room
18. t o b Architect, Killan Farmhouse
19. t o b Architect, Reuben Street
20. t o b Architect, The Quay

In Conversation
会話

We find meaning in the serendipities of circumstance. Architecture is called into being by needs in society, and shaped by forces, regulations, and materials that are often beyond our control. In this context we value conversation as a technique, as it leads onward, gathering idealized conceptions and contingent impositions into its ambit and finds form in a shared horizon.

In the making of our work the project always begins by response, in dialogue with what already exists – a response to the situation as found.

Clancy Moore Architects

思わぬ発見がたとえ巡り合わせによるものだとしても、私たちはそれを意義ある発見とみなす。建築は社会のニーズから生まれ、そして、私たちにはどうすることもできない諸般の影響や規制を受けつつ種々の素材によって具現される。ゆえに、私たちは会話の力に頼る。会話によって物事を前へ進め、諸々の理念を集約し、不慮の事態に対処してゆく——共通の地平にしかるべき形態を浮上させるべく。

私たちはどのプロジェクトでも必ず応答から、既存のものとの対話から始める。あるがままの状況に応じる、ということだ。(土居純訳)

クランシー・ムーア・アーキテクツ

Clancy Moore Architects
House on a Hill
Munster, Ireland 2018–2022

クランシー・ムーア・アーキテクツ
丘の上の家
アイルランド、マンスター 2018〜2022

建築と都市 ARCHITECTURE AND URBANISM 24:03

642

Feature:
Irish Architecture
20 Houses by 6 Architects

Clancy Moore Architects
House on a Hill
Munster, Ireland

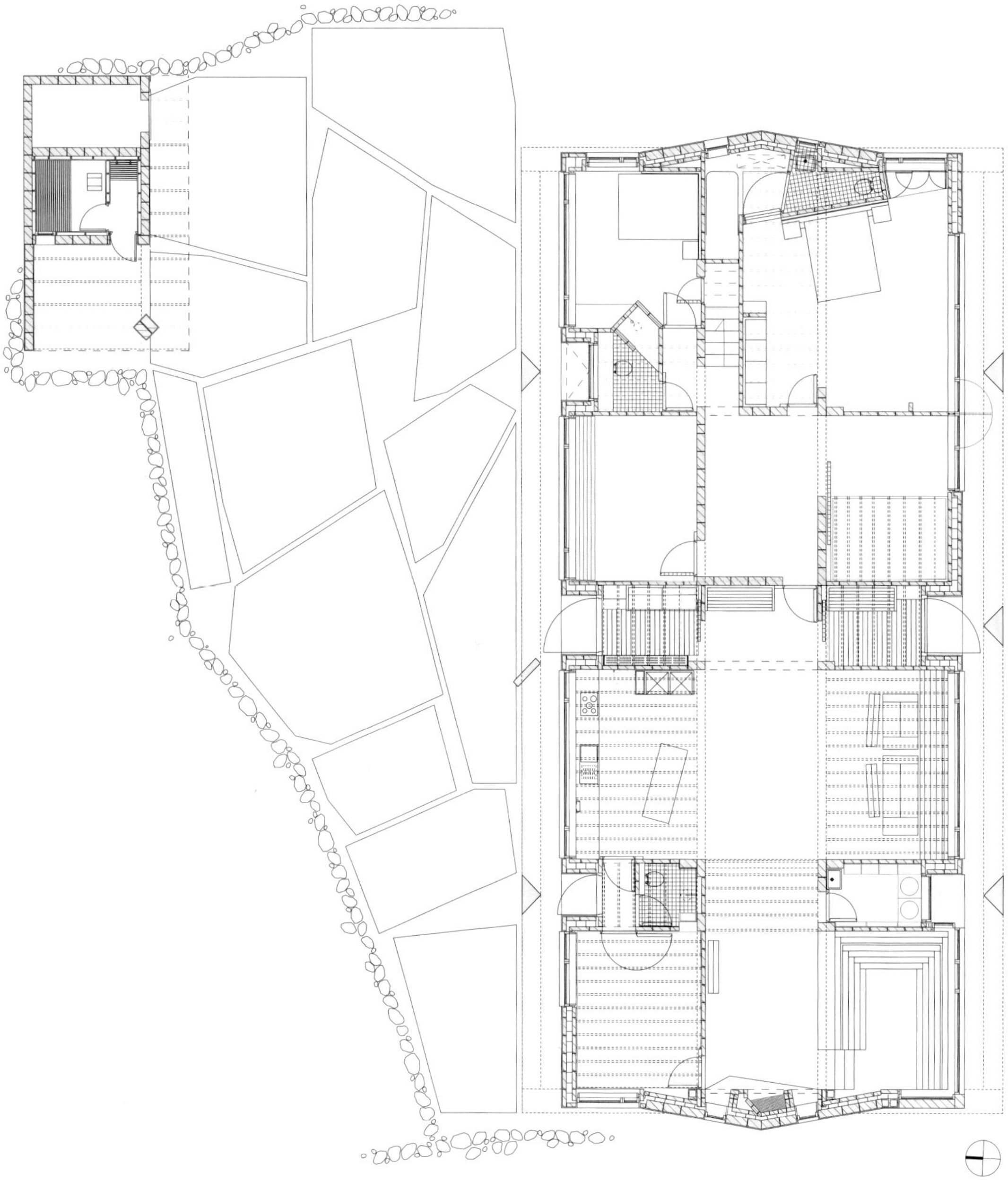

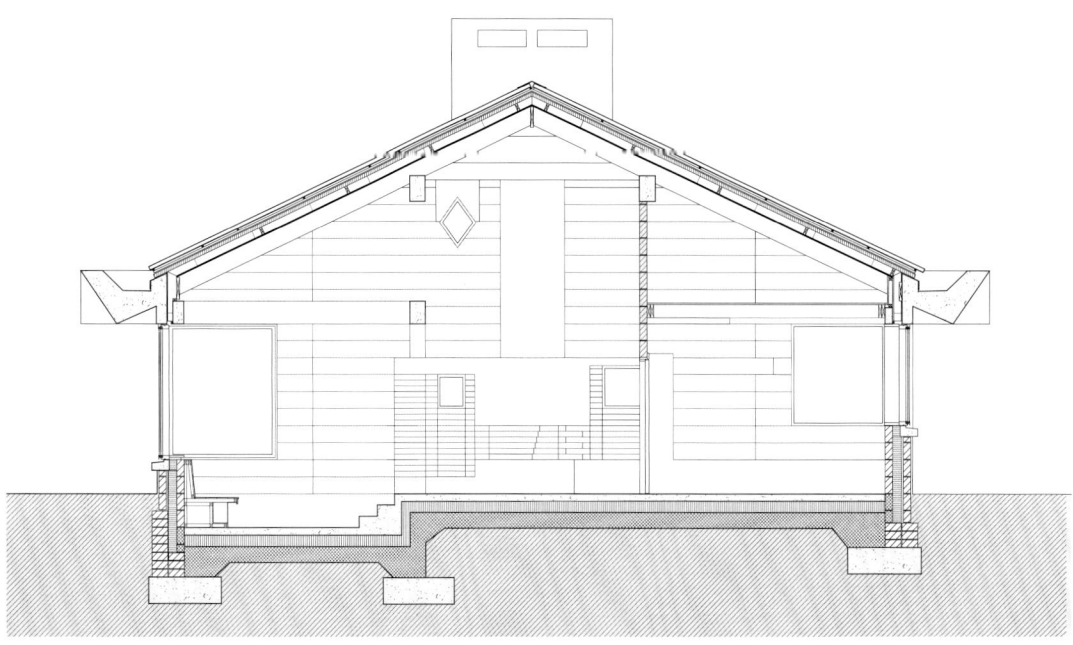

Ground-floor plan (scale: 1/180)／地上階平面図（縮尺：1/180）

Section (scale: 1/100)／断面図（縮尺：1/100）

This is a home for a family returning to Ireland. The client's brief was direct – create a place where a person can be on their own and not be lonely, and a place where they can still find quiet, even among a crowd.
With an interwoven organization of rooms and service spaces, the plan is all enfilade with no circulation. In places, this separation is eroded and inflected to allow for gregariousness and connection – with everything under an all-encompassing, fully inhabited roof that allows for intimate and monumental spaces, which weave across the plan.

これはアイルランドに帰ってきた家族のための住宅である。クライアントは簡潔に、自分のことをしながらひとりぼっちにならず、人が集まる中でも静寂を感じられる住宅を求めていた。
住宅平面は部屋とサーヴィス空間を編み目状に組みこんだ秩序をもち、全部屋が動線用の通路なしでつながる縦列配置となっている。この秩序はところどころで侵食され、屈折し、群居や接続を可能にする。あらゆるものは生活の全てを包む大屋根の下にあり、親密かつ記念碑的な空間がプランを紡いでいく。　　　　　　（松本晴子訳）

Credits and Data
Project title: House on a Hill
Client: Private
Location: Munster, Ireland
Design: 2018
Completion: 2022
Architects: Andrew Clancy, Colm Moore
Design team: Erang Park, David Magennis, Alexandra Pickerill
Project team: Brunner Engineers (engineering), Fordlin Construction (construction)
Site area: 4,000 m^2
Gross floor area: 235 m^2

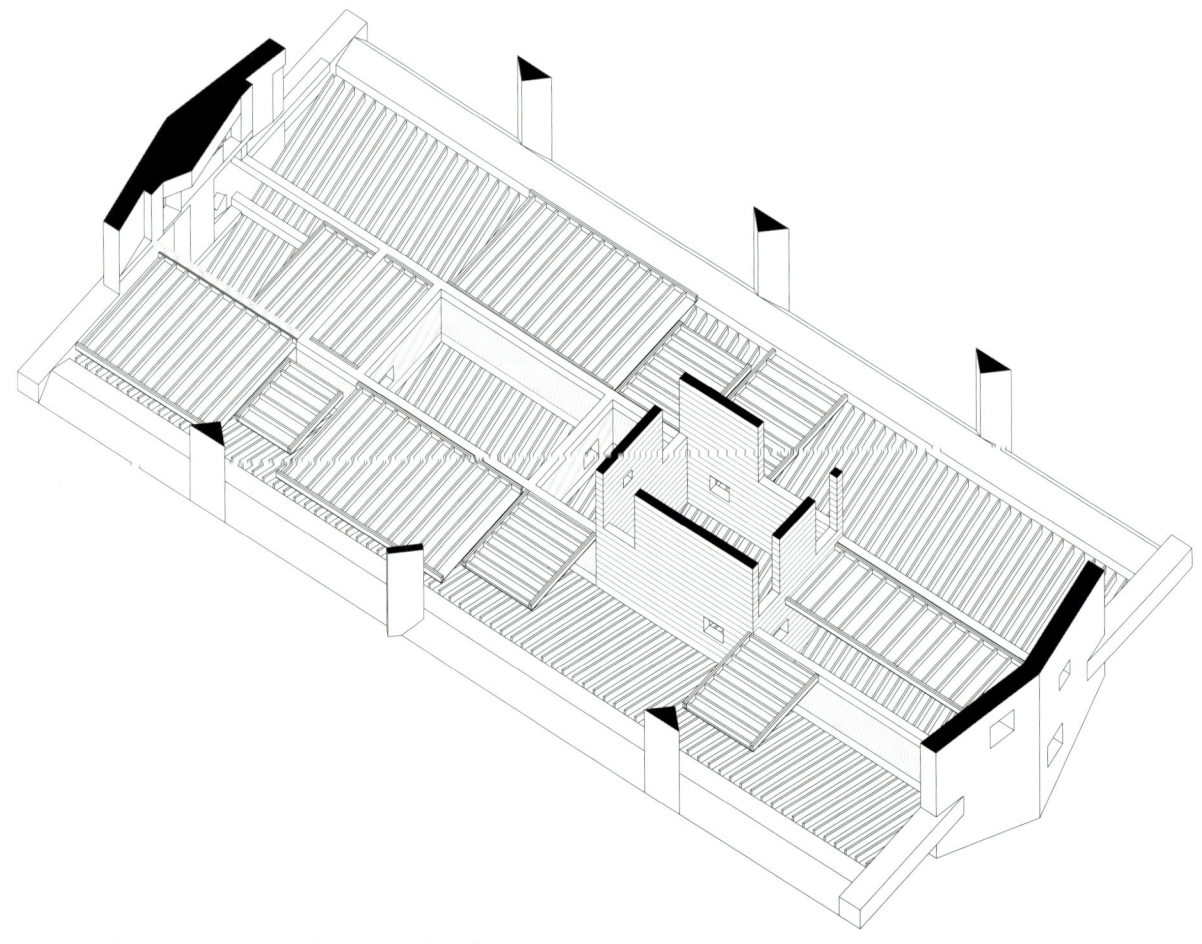

Inverted ceiling axonometric／天伏アクソノメトリック図

pp. 14–15: View of the house from the southeast within the surrounding landscape. Photos on pp. 14–19 by Noreile Breen. p. 16: East façade. p. 17: Shed on the north side of the site. p. 19: West façade. pp. 20–21: Ground-floor dining area. Photos on pp. 20–25 by Sue Barr. p. 22: Looking east from the ground-floor central hall. p. 23: The fireplace. Opposite: The fireplace is visible from the living room. This page: Built-in sofa in the living area.

14〜15頁：南東から住宅と周囲のランドスケープを見る。16頁：東ファサード。17頁：北側の小屋。19頁：西ファサード。20〜21頁：地上階ダイニング・スペース。22頁：地上階中央から住宅の東側を見る。23頁：暖炉のある居間スペース。左頁：一段下がった居間スペースから暖炉を見る。本頁：造付けのソファのある居間スペース。

Clancy Moore Architects
Mulgrave
Dublin, Ireland 2021–2022

クランシー・ムーア・アーキテクツ
マルグレイヴ
アイルランド、ダブリン　2021〜2022

建築と都市
ARCHITECTURE AND URBANISM
24:03

642

Feature:
Irish Architecture
20 Houses by 6 Architects

Clancy Moore Architects
Mulgrave
Dublin, Ireland

The existing building is a house on a terrace. Constructed in circa 1850, it is an unremarkable but elegant 3-bay, 2-storey structure with a gabled roof set behind a granite stone parapet. The family required a space larger than any that exists and had a desire to live between inside and outside, with the garden. Poorly considered additions to the house, constructed over the past 20 years, exacerbate their frustrations.

The northeastern orientation is difficult, with direct light lost to the rear façade by midday. Here the project – a study in zenithal light – begins. A table is set to the back of the existing house, with a ceiling hung from this structure, a tent below a table. Light enters either side of it, drawn from above, afternoon and evening sunlight held on rough render. Structural columns are located asymmetrically as dictated by opposing openings to the rooms of the house and garden. Columns dance on the weathering line standing along the midpoint of support to the inner and outer plane of the cavity wall construction. Due to the existing topography, the back garden is sunken and overlooked. A new cornice is made to the garden framing the sky, which affords a sense of privacy. The garden thus becomes a room, and its cornice becomes a beam that prevents the existing rear granite wall from toppling over. A curved wall forms a new boundary to one side of the garden with utility spaces concealed in the thickness between wall and neighbors.

The resulting plan of rooms is deep and convivial, moderating spaces for the community of family alongside rooms for individual retreat – the existing and new drawn together as an enfilade formed in light.

Credits and Data
Project title: Mulgrave
Client: Private
Location: Dublin, Ireland
Design: 2021
Completion: 2022
Architects: Andrew Clancy, Colm Moore
Design team: Erang Park, Tobias Beale, Alexandra Pickerill
Project team: Brunner Engineers (engineering), Fordlin Construction (construction)
Site area: 1,000 m²
Gross floor area: 215 m²

高台に既存の住宅があった。1850年頃に建てられ、3つの柱間をもつ2階建煉瓦造の優美な建物であり、花崗岩の欄干後ろに切妻屋根が架けられている。家族は、既存の部屋よりも大きな空間を求めており、内と外の間で庭を使って暮らしたいと願っていた。過去20年間住宅になされてきた増築によって、家族の不満はさらに募っていた。
真昼になると裏ファサード側には直射日光が入らないため、北東は難しい。天頂光の研究としてのこのプロジェクトはここから始まった。既存住宅の奥にはテーブルが一台置かれており、天井が構造から吊り下げられている。テーブルの下にはテントがある。その両側上方から引き込まれた光が、午後から夕暮れにかけてざらついた壁面に注ぎ込む。構造柱は、内部の部屋と庭の開口が対になるよう、左右非対称に配置されている。柱は、中空壁構造の内外の中間点に立ち、風化の線上で踊りを舞う。裏庭は地形のせいで日当たりが悪く、見晴らしが悪い。庭には新たなコーニスが設けられ、空を縁取ることで私的な感覚がもたらされた。こうして庭は部屋となり、コーニスは梁となり、背後の花崗岩の既存壁の倒壊を防いでいる。庭の一方にもうけられた曲壁が新たな境界線をつくり、設備空間が隣家との間の厚みの中に「隠されて」いる。
結果、奥行きのあるくつろげる部屋がもたらされ、家族という共同体のための空間と、個々人の隠れ家が共存する。こうして既存部と新築部が光でできた縦列配置として一体化した。
(松本晴子訳)

p. 26: The exterior of the original house. An addition on the north side increased the interior space. Photos on pp. 26–28 by Noreile Breen unless otherwise specified. p. 27: The courtyard where the extension was built. This page, bottom left: The house seen from the courtyard. This page, bottom right: During construction. Photo courtesy of Clancy Moore Architects.

26頁：元の住宅外壁を見る。北側に増築がなされ、内部空間が追加された。27頁：増築された部屋から中庭を見る。本頁、左下：中庭から住宅を見る。本頁、右下：施工時。

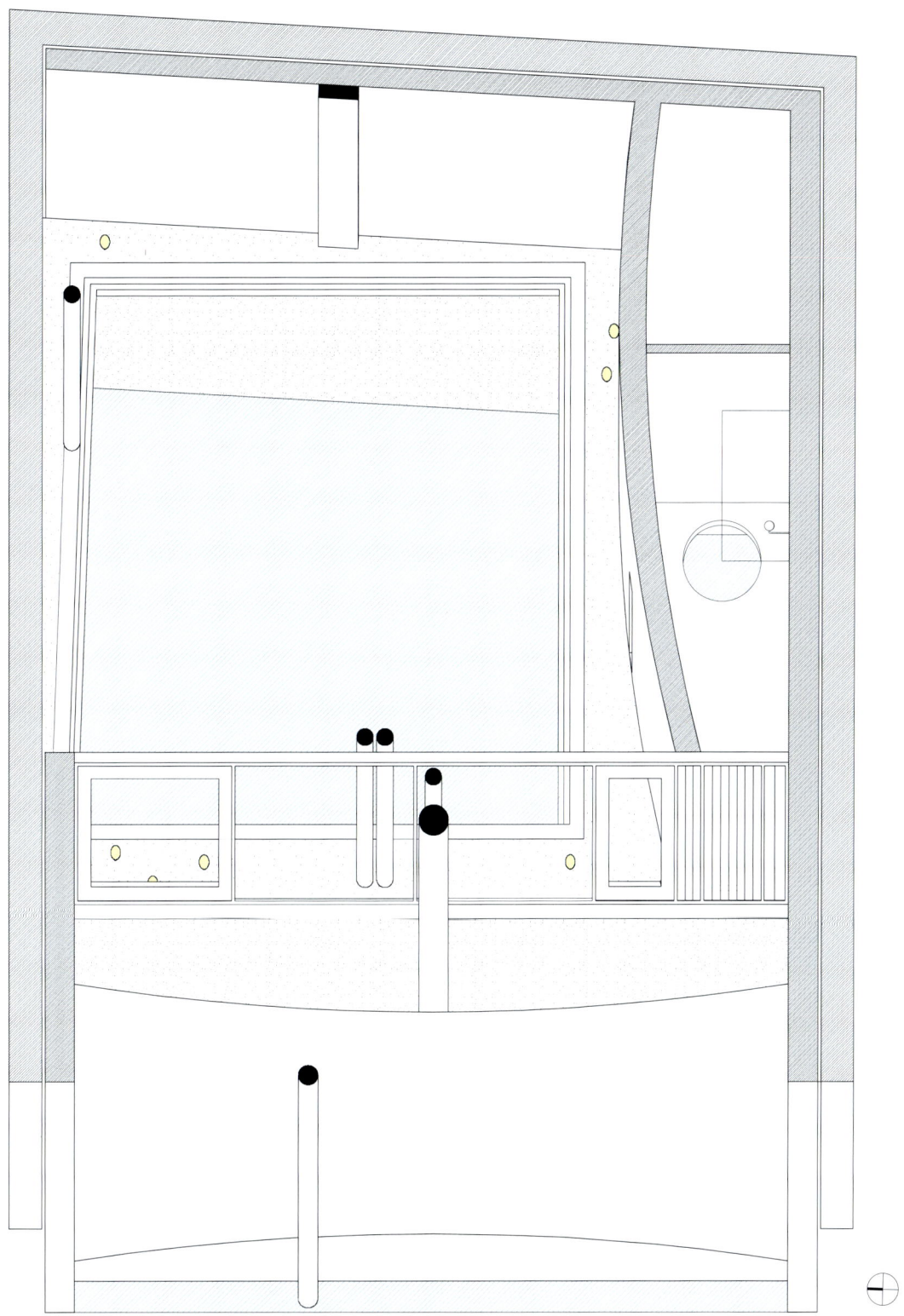

Inverted ceiling axonometric／天伏アクソノメトリック図

Clancy Moore Architects
Ailesbury
Dublin, Ireland 2019–2021

クランシー・ムーア・アーキテクツ
アイルズベリー
アイルランド、ダブリン　2019〜2021

For this project we renovated a previously modified Victorian house. Our work to the rear is less an addition than a weaving, building on a careful consideration of the site as we found it. A series of deep and low-ceiling rooms here made for a dark and unusable heart to the house – the only resonant space offered was a PVC bay window, in disrepair. We enjoyed its ambiguity – both the way a bay window can be part of, yet apart from, a larger room and the external space captured within the fold of its geometry. This ambiguity between inside and outside and the individual within a community was part of the conversation with our clients when we discussed how they might inhabit the large family room they wanted as the center of their new home.

We saw our addition to the existing property as an elaborated bay window. A series of bay windows and roof lights implies rooms of various scales in a large open plan. The rear wall of the house is propped at the first-floor level by a steel column that opens the existing rooms to the back of the house as one large living space. This structural figure anchors the spaces surrounding it. In spite of being part of a terrace, each of these "rooms," for cooking, gathering, eating, and relaxing, is lit from all directions. A geometry of bay windows and roof lights drawing light deep into the plan creates open, long views, sometimes to the garden outside and other times to other rooms in the house.

Credits and Data
Project title: Ailesbury
Client: Private
Location: Dublin, Ireland
Design: 2019
Completion: 2021
Architects: Andrew Clancy, Colm Moore
Design team: Erang Park, Marc Golden, David Magennis.
Project team: Brunner Engineers (engineering), Fordlin Construction (construction)
Site area: 700 m^2
Gross floor area: 295 m^2

pp. 30–31: Exterior of the extension. Photos on pp. 30–34 by Fionn McCann. p. 32: Dining space. p. 33: Living space. This page, bottom left: The kitchen, abutting the existing building, has the original overhanging window above. This page, bottom right: The hallway has a series of round windows.

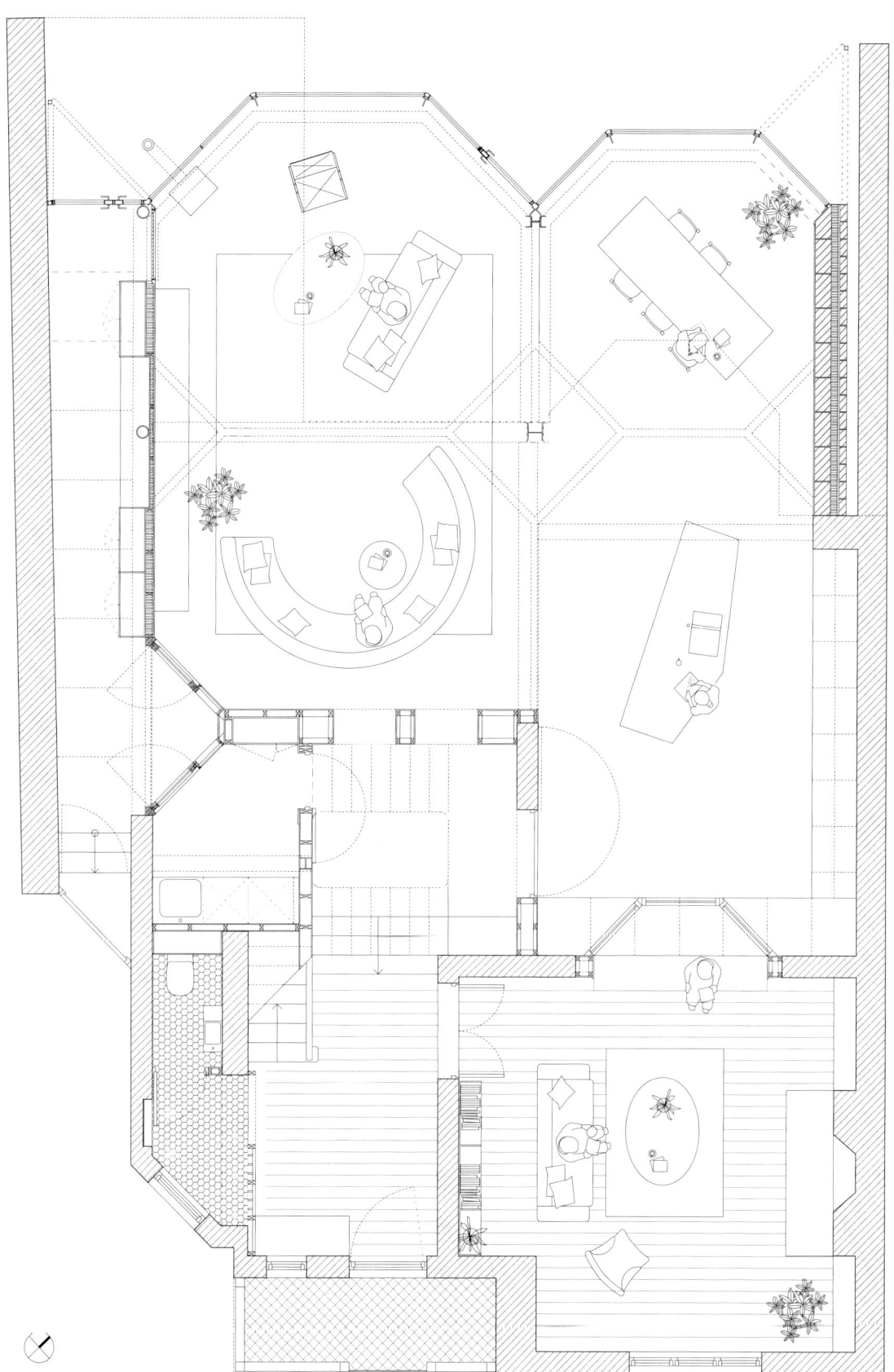

Ground-floor plan (scale: 1/80)／地上階平面図（縮尺：1/80）

Clancy Moore Architects
Writers Room
Dublin, Ireland 2019–2020

クランシー・ムーア・アーキテクツ
小説家の部屋
アイルランド、ダブリン　2019〜2020

This project arose during the COVID-19 lockdown, to make a space for a novelist to write in solitude in his garden. With the site behind an existing terrace of houses, and inaccessible to builders, we designed the room so it could be constructed off-site and craned into position. This aspect governed the design, meaning it became an exercise in *éspace minimum* (minimal space), for its weight to work with the capacity of the crane. This weight limit also helped once the building was in position, allowing us to avoid conventional foundations in favor of augured ground anchors that could be screwed into the soil. The form, too, was shaped by these limits, with the room having an exoskeleton that allowed it to be hung when in motion and to sit on its foundations once in position.

With these contingencies we found space for a rich internal world, lined in red-stained beech and mirror. It provides a desk to work from, and a daybed to rest. Placed in a corner of the garden, the room seeks to capture a series of spaces between itself and the surrounding planting. Reflecting the idea that repose is as important as production, the room reaches beyond the site via its mirrored ceiling, which provides a distant view from the daybed to the sea.

このプロジェクトはロックダウンの最中に生まれた。小説家が孤独に執筆するための空間として自宅の庭に設けられた。敷地は家々が立ち並ぶテラスの背後にあり、重機を入れることができなかったため、敷地外で建設し、クレーンで移動、所定の位置に設置できるようデザインを行なった。この点がデザインを支配する要素となり、クレーンで対応できる重量の最小限空間を設計することとなった。重量制限は、建物の配置後にも役にたち、従来の基礎ではなく、土にねじこむオーガー式地中アンカーを採用することが可能になった。形態も重量制限によって決定された。部屋は外骨格からなり、吊るして動かすことが可能になり、所定の位置で基礎の上に着地する。

これらの偶発性の中から、赤く塗装したブナ材と鏡の並んだ豊かな内的世界がみいだされた。机があるので仕事もでき、ソファベッドで休息をとることもできる。庭の一角に置かれたこの部屋は、周囲の植栽との間に連続した空間をつくりだそうとしている。休息は執筆と同等に重要であることを認識することで、部屋は敷地を越えて広がり、ソファベッドから、天井に張った鏡を通して、海を遠く眺めることができる。

（松本晴子訳）

Opposite: Close-up of the opening that shows the red painted beechwood interior. Photos on pp. 37–39 Fionn McCann. p. 38: Installation. p. 39, top: Interior. p. 39, bottom: Entrance.

右頁：外壁のクロースアップ、内装は赤く塗装されたブナ材で仕上げられた。38頁：設置中の様子。39頁、上：内観。39頁、下：エントランス。

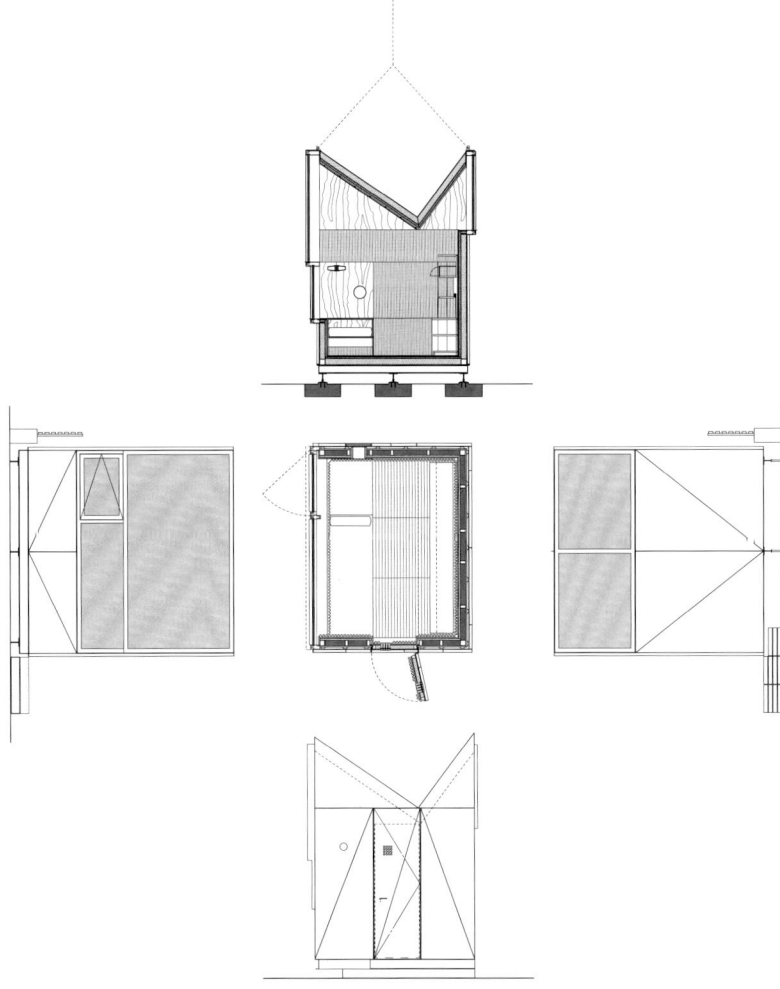

Plan, section, elevations (scale: 1/120)／平立断面図（縮尺：1/120）

Credits and Data
Project title: Writers Room
Client: Private
Location: Dublin, Ireland
Design: 2019
Completion: 2020
Architects: Andrew Clancy, Colm Moore
Design team: Erang Park, David Magennis
Project team: Brunner Engineers (engineering), Fordlin Construction (construction)
Site area: 500 m^2
Gross floor area: 9 m^2

Space between Notes

音の空白

Tunes in an oral tradition are short-form compositional objects, like poems. The interior of a tune is important to trying to understand its overall character – rich subsets of interdependent compositional relationships across multiple scales of detail. These tunes have an apparent simplicity that often belies their complex interiors. Similarly, in architecture, we establish relationships between different elements in a way that offers syntax, character, and meaning. When sensitive to the cultural context, these relationships work outward to landscape.

Steve Larkin Architects

口頭伝承の調べは、詩にも似た短い形式をとる。その調べの内面に注目してはじめて、曲の性格を理解できる──部分部分の相互依存的関係が大小の細部を豊かに響かせているのだ。こうした調べはいかにも単純そうに見えてそのじつ、複雑な内面を隠しもつ。同じく建築においても私たちは、個々の要素を互いに結びつけることで建築に構文（構造）と性格と意味を付与する。現地の文化的背景に敏感であれば、この結びつきが周囲の風景にもおのずから波及する。（土居純訳）

スティーヴ・ラーキン・アーキテクツ

Steve Larkin Architects
House at Ballyblake
Ballyblake, Ireland 2016–2021

スティーヴ・ラーキン・アーキテクツ
バリーブレイクの家
アイルランド、バリーブレイク　2016〜2021

Ballyblake House is a 200-year-old farmhouse on a secluded site that is embedded within a dense pattern of laneways, fields, and hedgerows in an old agricultural landscape near the picturesque village of Saint Mullin's in county Carlow. Our project principally sought to protect the character of this place – to preserve the agricultural patterns of development, the hedgerows, laneways, the building enclave around the house, the house itself, and their relationships to the surrounding landscape.

The house and site were derelict and had been uninhabited for over 30 years. Despite challenges with the condition and original construction, we carefully refurbished the house and landscape to maintain the existing spatial relationships on the site and preserve its personal, historical, and cultural significance.

The house was fully renovated to protect the original construction. A new timber frame extension, which evolves a language from characteristics of local farm buildings, is placed behind the existing house to minimize spatial impact and open new views to the wider landscape – facilitated by rebuilding a hedgerow and replanting 2 ash trees. The new extension blankets the original house to the north for improved thermal performance, while an oculus provides sunlight to the interior spaces throughout the day.

バリーブレイクの家は人里離れた場所にある築200年の農家であり、カーロウ県の絵のように美しいセント・マリンズ村にほど近い、古い農村風景のなかにある。小道、畑、生垣のパターンが入り組んだ中に位置する。我々は場所の特徴を守ることを第一に優先した。発展過程を示す農地のパターン、生垣、小道、建物の囲い、家そのもの、そして周囲のランドスケープとの関係を保存することであった。

住宅と敷地は廃墟と化しており30年以上人が住んでいなかった。その状態や既存建物が抱えていた問題にもかかわらず、住宅とランドスケープは慎重に改修された。敷地内に元々あった空間関係は維持され、個人・歴史・文化的意義を残すことが目指された。オリジナルの建物を保護するため、全面的な改修が行われた。木構造の増築は、地元の農家建物がもつ建築言語からの発展であり、空間への影響を最小限に抑えて広範なランドスケープに新しい眺望を開くため、既存住宅の奥に配置された。生垣をつくり直し、2本のトネリコの木を植え替えることで実現された。増築部は北の既存住宅を覆って熱性能を向上させ、円形の天窓からは内部空間に一日中太陽光が注ぎ込む。

（松本晴子訳）

This page: The house seen in the distance. Photos on pp. 42–49 by Shantanu Starick. Opposite: Close-up of the roof, which covers the connection to the existing house.

本頁：遠景。右頁：屋根とファサードのクロースアップ。奥に見える屋根は既存住宅との接続部を覆う。

Credits and Data
Project title: House at Ballyblake
Client: Thelma Cantlon and Dave Murtagh
Location: Ballyblake, Marley, county Carlow, Ireland
Design: 2016
Completion: 2021
Architects: Steve Larkin, Deepka Abbi
Project team: David Maher (structure), Seosamh Lalor (construction), PJ Lalor (carpentry and furniture), PJ Dunbar (joinery)
Site area: 7,200 m²
Gross floor area: 230 m²

建築と都市
ARCHITECTURE AND URBANISM
24:03

642

Feature:
Irish Architecture
20 Houses by 6 Architects

Steve Larkin Architects
House at Ballyblake
Ballyblake, Ireland

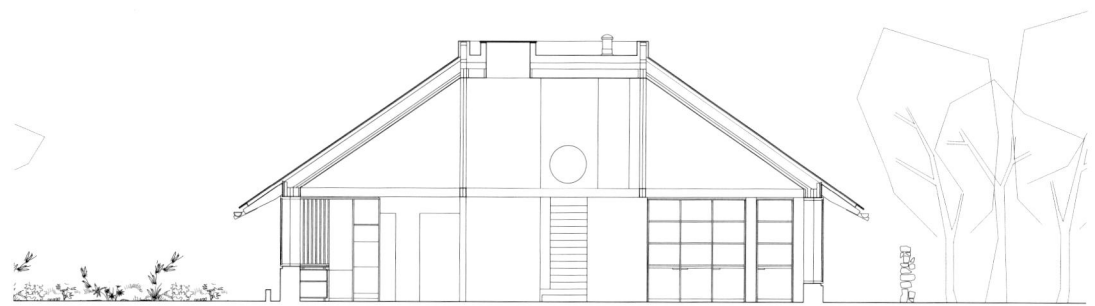

Section (scale: 1/180)／断面図（縮尺：1/180）

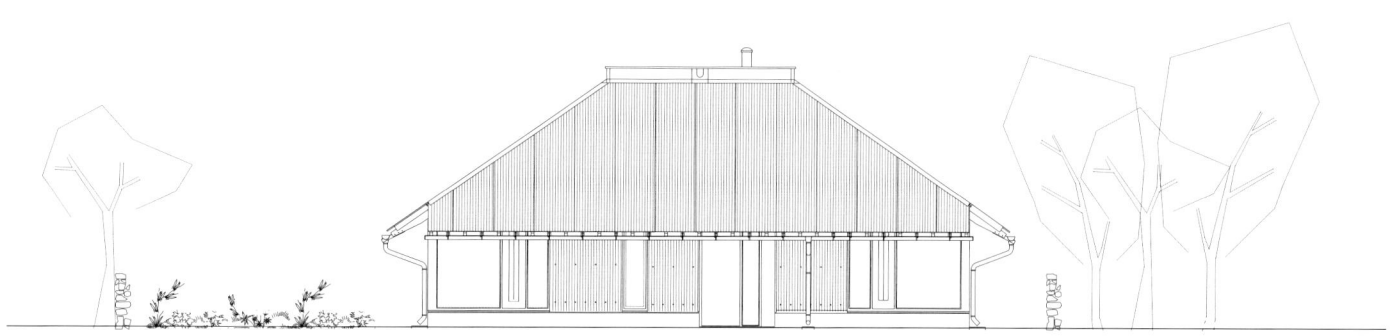

North elevation／北立面図

South elevation (scale: 1/180)／南立面図（縮尺：1/180）

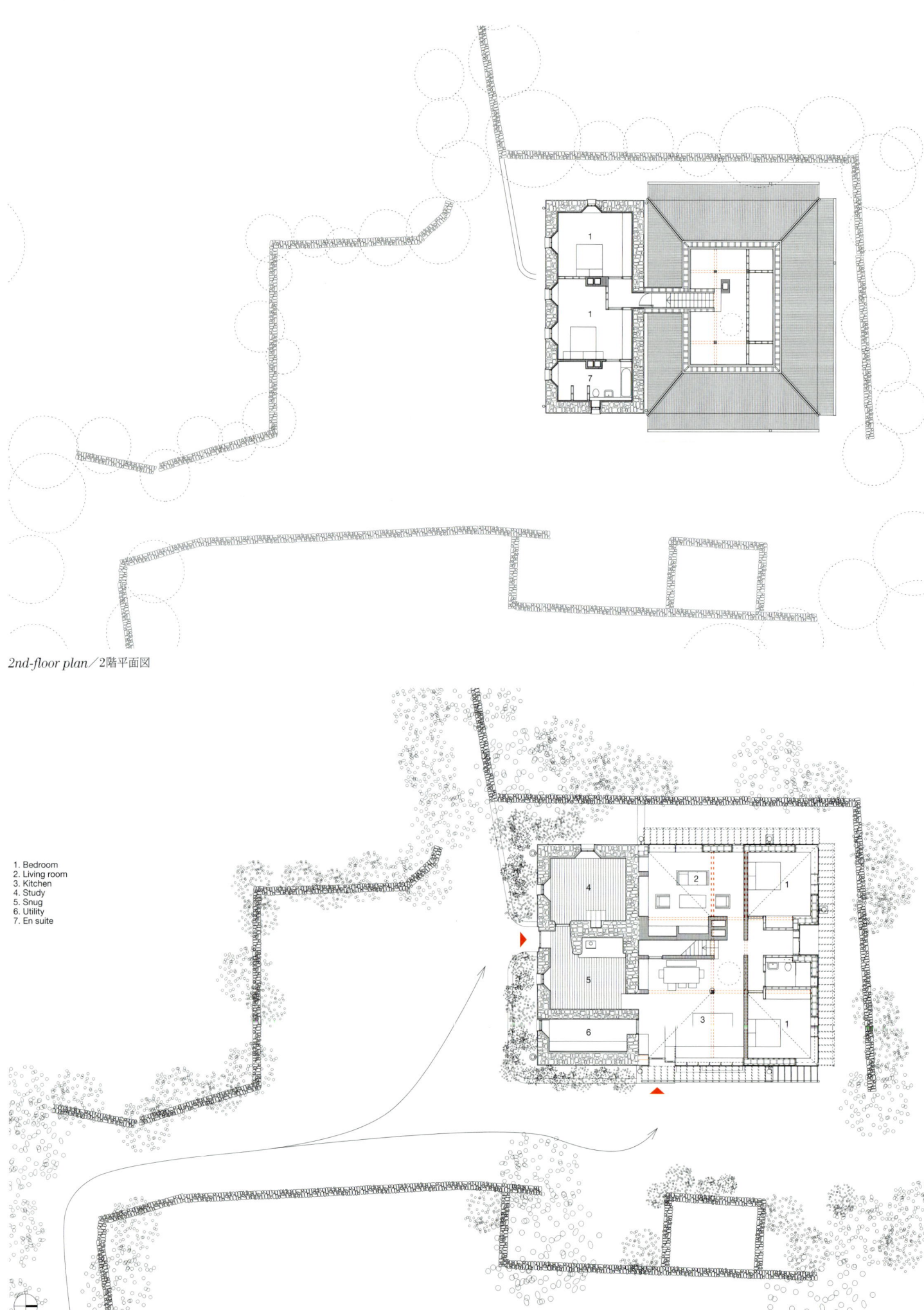

2nd-floor plan／2階平面図

1. Bedroom
2. Living room
3. Kitchen
4. Study
5. Snug
6. Utility
7. En suite

Ground-floor plan (scale: 1/300)／地上階平面図（縮尺：1/300）

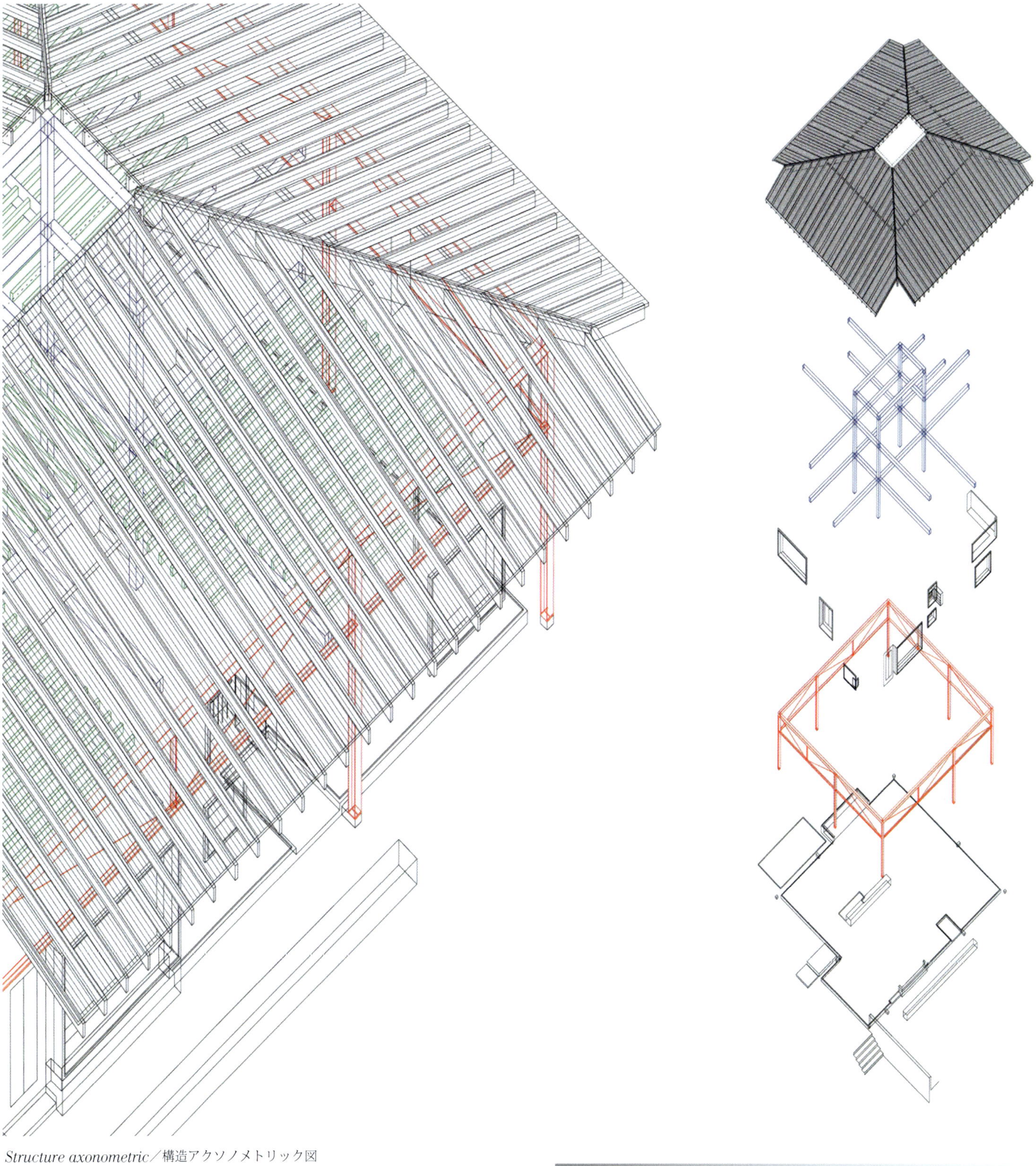

Structure axonometric／構造アクソノメトリック図

p. 44: Northwest corner. p. 46: The kitchen in the east seen from the center of the room p. 47: Stairs lead to the existing house. p. 48: Bedroom. p. 49: Kitchen and entrance. This page: Model. Photo courtesy of Steve Larkin Architects.

44頁：北西の角を見る。46頁：室内中央から東側のキッチンを見る。47頁：既存住宅につながる階段を右に見る。48頁：寝室。49頁：キッチンとエントランス。本頁：模型。

Steve Larkin Architects
House at Bogwest
Bogwest, Ireland 2008–2011

スティーヴ・ラーキン・アーキテクツ
ボグウェストの家
アイルランド、ボグウェスト　2008〜2011

642

ARCHITECTURE AND URBANISM
24:03

Feature:
Irish Architecture
20 Houses by 6 Architects

Steve Larkin Architects
House at Bogwest
Bogwest, Ireland

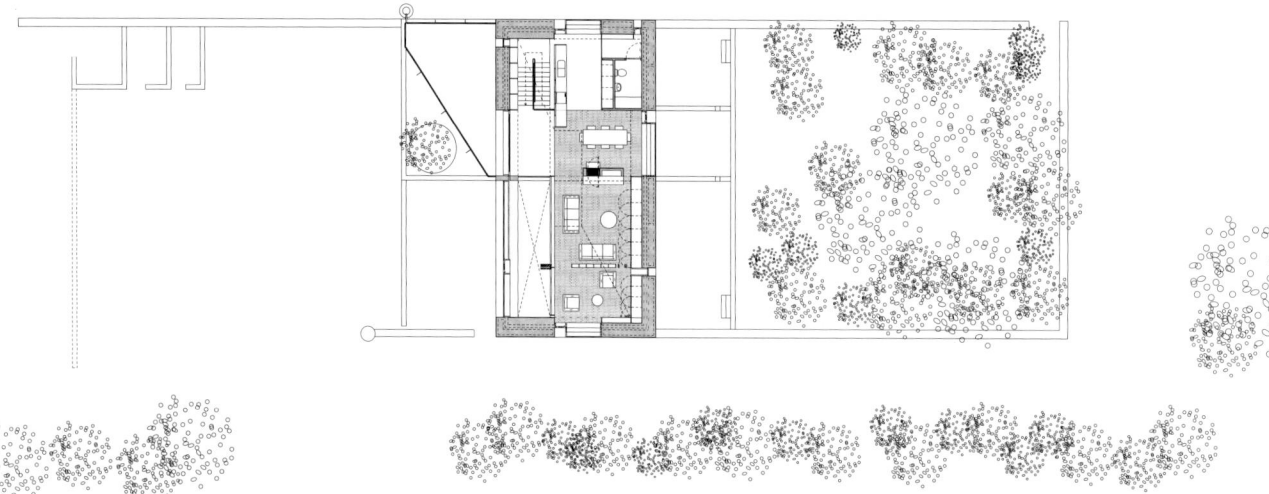

2nd-floor plan／2階平面図

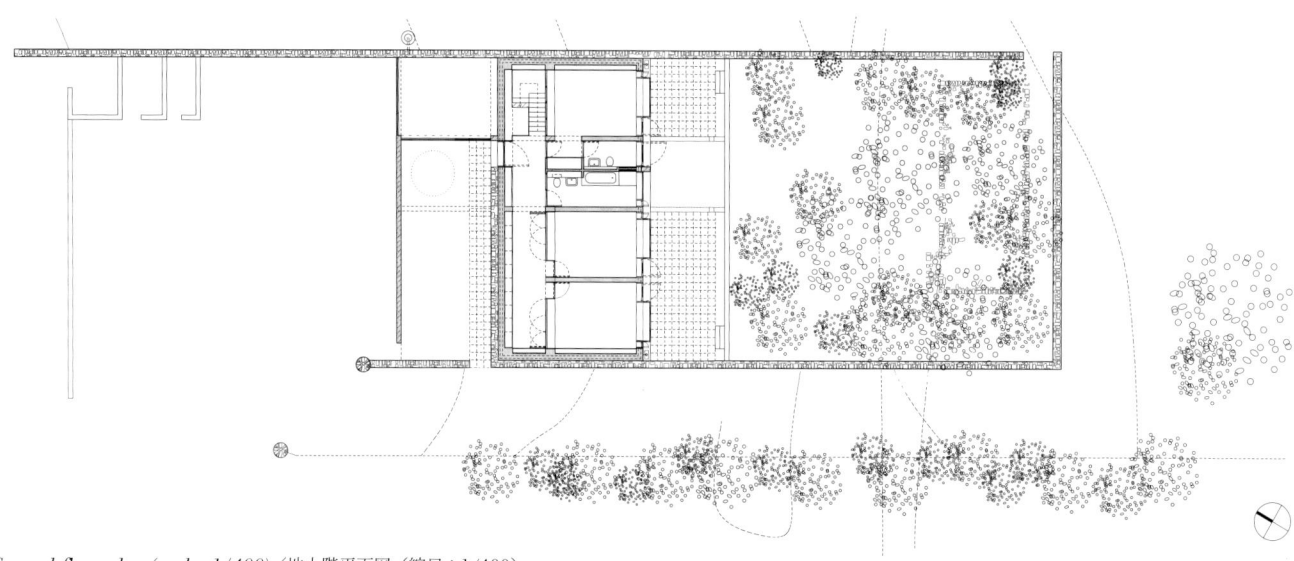

Ground-floor plan (scale: 1/400)／地上階平面図（縮尺：1/400）

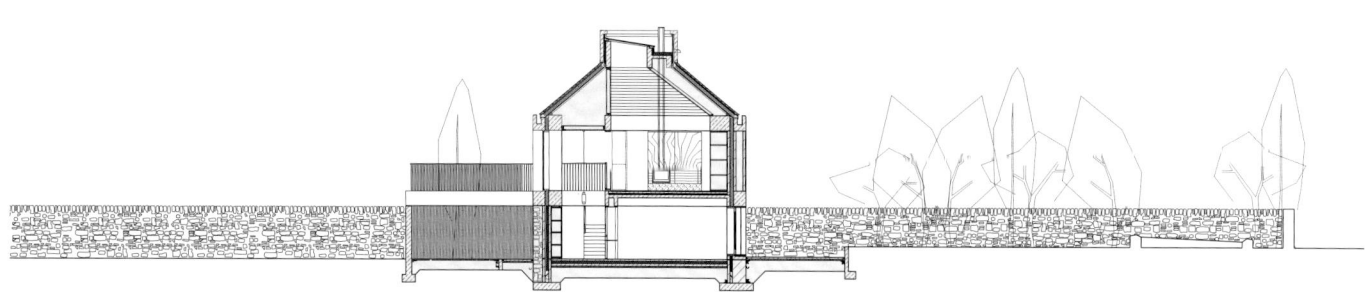

Section (scale: 1/300)／断面図（縮尺：1/300）

Built inside a ruined farmyard enclave of laneways, walls, and sheds, this house is positioned within these ruins to make multiple external spaces – a new entrance court, an enclosed garden, a laneway, and a parking area – and to enjoy the remarkable views across south county Wexford. The internal accommodation is arranged around these spaces. Bedrooms have privacy at ground level with an intimate relationship to the enclosed garden. Living areas on the second floor have openness and a view. The roof light illuminates these living areas throughout the day, while the section is nuanced to ensure no spaces are alienated from the ground.

A 3-leaf wall construction integrates the existing stone walls into the external wall construction. Bay windows within this wall thickness have deeply recessed opening lights, and a contemporary cornice detail can easily be accommodated within this thickness. In the enclosed garden, the joinery work of the bay windows becomes explicit.

The cultural context is important, as the house is a contemporary adaptation of the classical house of the middle size, reinterpreting architectural detailing and landscape relationship. Construction details prioritize economy, compositional balance, and local materials and building practices.

Credits and Data
Project title: House at Bogwest
Client: Paul Conlon and Clare Williams
Location: Bogwest, Mayglass, county Wexford, Ireland
Design: 2008
Completion: 2011
Architect: Steve Larkin
Project team: Arthur Murphy (structure), Martin Brennan (construction), PJ Dunbar (joinery), PJ Brady (furniture)
Site area: 9,300 m^2
Gross floor area: 200 m^2

p. 52: The 2nd-floor living space. Photos on pp. 52–57 by Alice Clancy. p. 53: Southeast façade. p. 54: The 2nd-floor dining space. p. 55: The Staircase leading from the ground-floor bedrooms to the 2nd-floor common space. This page, bottom left: Ground-floor bedrooms. This page, bottom right: The atrium.

Steve Larkin Architects
House at Slyguff
Slyguff, Ireland 2014–2019

スティーヴ・ラーキン・アーキテクツ
スライガフの家
アイルランド、スライガフ　2014〜2019

建築と都市
ARCHITECTURE AND URBANISM
24:03

642

Feature:
Irish Architecture
20 Houses by 6 Architects

Steve Larkin Architects
House at Slyguff
Slyguff, Ireland

This house is located on a family farm in the historic Slyguff landscape in county Carlow. The client's family has curated this landscape for generations, and they continue to play an important role in the conservation of its natural, cultural, and archaeological character. Now the home enables the younger generation to continue this tradition.
Context is very important. Cultural artifacts, with origins in farming, archaeology, neoclassicism, Victorian industry, and infrastructure, contribute significantly to the spatial character of this landscape. While this house seeks to integrate into this spatial character, it also establishes new relationships with these contextual artifacts.
The house is both a singular object in the landscape and elements that form an assemblage. At the landscape scale, a strong geometry is set against the undulating farmland and the archetypal geometry of the adjacent ringfort. An inverted plinth, which integrates the house into the site, makes a space in the landscape resemble the ringfort. At the project scale, the warm envelope is weathered by a cast-in-situ concrete outer shell. The collection of elements – such as rainfall gutters, windows, gables, columns, tapestry ceilings, plinths, greenhouses, and gargoyles – provide opportunities for space and syntactical order.
By providing the intimate and social spaces of the house, the ground floor emphasizes companionship and interiority within the larger landscape. Perched above the topography, the attic provides a studio / play space with views of the landscape through 2 ocular windows. Windows with low-level eaves capture light and rain in the attic.

この住宅は家族経営の農場に位置しており、カーロウ県の歴史あるスライガフのランドスケープに囲まれている。クライアントは数世代にわたってここを管理してきた家族の一員であり、自然・文化・考古学的な風土の保護に携わっている。この住宅は、若い世代がこうした伝統を引き継ぐことを可能にする。
コンテクストは非常に重要である。農業、考古学、新古典主義、ヴィクトリア朝時代の産業やインフラに由来する文化遺物はこのランドスケープの空間的特徴に大きく貢献している。この住宅はこうした空間に溶け込んでおり、コンテクストを形成する遺物と新たな関係を築こうとしている。
住宅は、ランドスケープにおける唯一のオブジェであると同時に、要素の集合でもある。ランドスケープ規模においては、起伏のある農地と、隣の円形土砦のもつ原型的幾何学にたいし、力強い幾何学がデザインされた。逆さの台座は、住宅を円形土砦のようなランドスケープ空間に統合する。プロジェクト規模においては、暖かな外被は場所打ちコンクリートの外部シェルによって風化している。雨樋、窓、妻壁、柱、タペストリー天井、台座、温室、ガーゴイルなど、要素の集合が空間と統語論的秩序の機会をもたらしている。
地上階は親密かつ社交的な空間を提供しており、広範なランドスケープにおいての人との交流と内部性を強調する。屋根裏はアトリエや遊び場となり、地面より高い位置にあるため、2つの丸窓からは風景が眺められる。低い軒下窓は屋根裏の光と雨をとり込む。
（松本晴子訳）

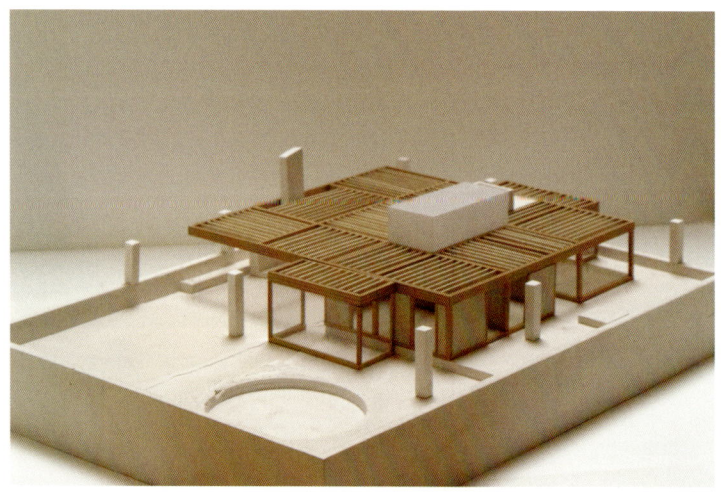

pp. 58–59: The house seen from the south. Photos on pp. 58–59, 66–67 by Alice Clancy. p. 60: Longitudinal façade. Photos on pp. 60–65, 69 by Shantanu Starick. p. 61: Southwest façade. This page, bottom: Model. Opposite: South corner of the building.

58〜59頁：南から見る。60頁：平側ファサード。61頁：南西ファサード。本頁、下：構造模型。右頁：南側の角。

Credits and Data
Project title: House at Slyguff
Client: Justin and Adéle Kidd
Location: Slyguff, Muine Bheag, county Carlow, Ireland
Design: 2014
Completion: 2019
Architects: Steve Larkin, Deepka Abbi, Noreile Breen
Project team: Arthur Murphy (structure), Ivor Bowe (site survey and soil testing), Martin Brennan (concrete), Drumore Construction Ltd (general construction), PJ Brady (furniture)
Site area: 3,700 m²
Gross floor area: 285 m²

p. 64: The kitchen seen from the living room. p. 65: Kitchen and dining area. pp. 66–67: 2nd floor living area. Opposite: View from the 2nd-floor.

64頁：北側の居間から対角線上のキッチン・ダイニングを見る。65頁：キッチン・ダイニング。66〜67頁：2階内観。左頁：2階の開口からランドスケープを望む。

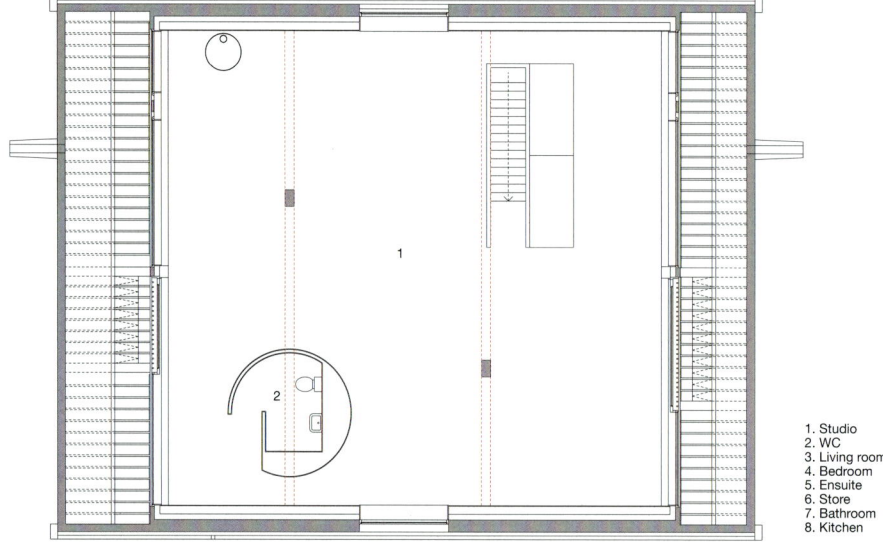

1. Studio
2. WC
3. Living room
4. Bedroom
5. Ensuite
6. Store
7. Bathroom
8. Kitchen

2nd-floor plan／2階平面図

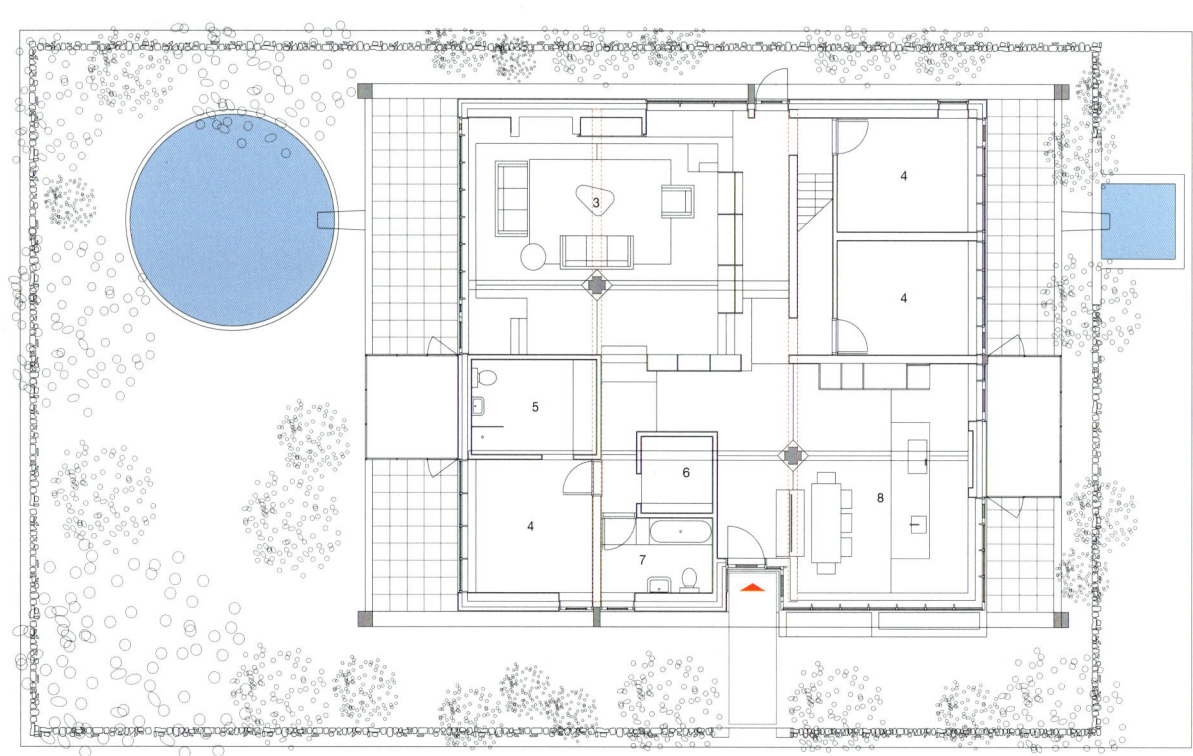

Ground-floor plan (scale: 1/200)／地上階平面図（縮尺：1/200）

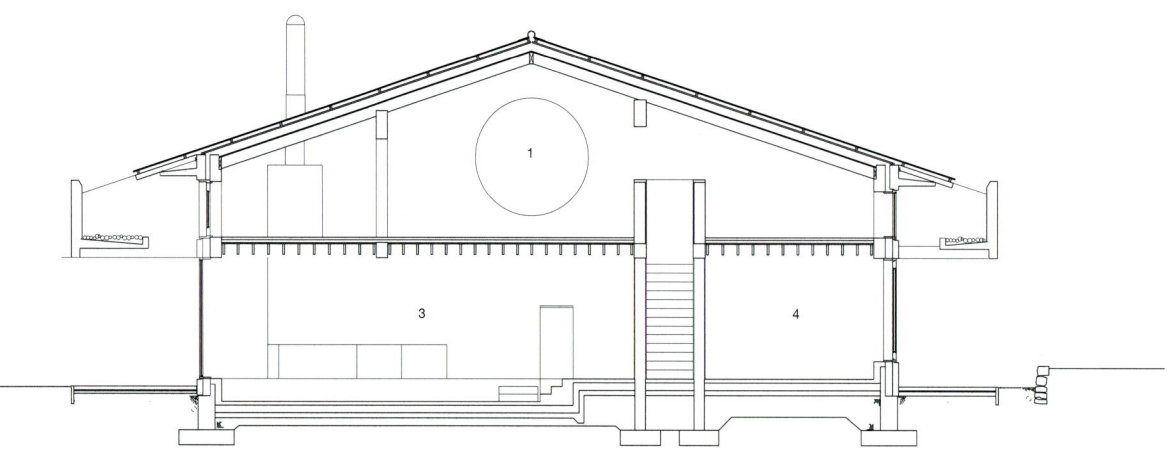

Section (scale: 1/150)／断面図（縮尺：1/150）

Future Pasts

未来に生き続ける過去

A local culture of building exists everywhere in the ordinary structures that make up the character of the built environment, in the typical forms of houses, the standard construction methods, the usual materials, the everyday windows, and so forth. The greatest opportunity for richness of experience and depth of intelligibility will stem from a local building language. Our architecture is situated within this web of interconnected patterns past and present, evoking memory and meaning for those indwelled.

Ryan W. Kennihan Architects

地域の建物文化というものは、その土地のいたるところに残っている。たとえば、現地の構築環境を性格づけているごく普通の建物であるとか、典型的な住宅形態や、標準的な工法、ありきたりの素材、平凡な窓などに。建物が人に豊かな体験を与え、深く理解されるための格好の条件とは、現地の建物言語を基調とすることだろう。私たちの建築は、過去と未来とが絡み合った網の目の内にあって、そこに暮らす者の記憶と想像を喚起する。(土居純訳)

ライアン・W・ケニハン・アーキテクツ

Ryan W. Kennihan Architects
Dromlee House
Dublin, Ireland 2020–2022

ライアン・W・ケニハン・アーキテクツ
ドロムリー・ハウス
アイルランド、ダブリン　2020〜2022

Outside of Dublin's core of predominantly Georgian and Victorian architecture lies a near continuous ring of suburban mid-20th-century single-family houses, densely packed as row houses, or "semidetached," pairs. These neighborhoods are predominantly constructed very affordably in concrete block, cement plaster, and roof tiles. While most of these houses have limited exterior spaces, occasionally, by a happy accident of cul-de-sac geometries, a large angular garden can be found. Our clients acquired one such secret garden with a wedge shape that meets the street at the width of a car while it widens to 23 m at the rear. So, while the project's goal was to double the size of the small existing house, it also emphasized connecting to the unique site.

The resulting design of a long slender block divides the site to create 2 types of garden: a smaller, shady entrance space and a rear sunny garden containing a green, raised beds, and a small orchard. To address this landscape, we designed a formal façade, which emphasizes the unusually wide site with windows aligned front and back and a new large hallway that connects the 2 gardens.

Constructed of the ordinary materials of the neighborhood, the house has a commonly found crisp plaster base. Its pebbledash (small stones mixed with wet plaster) top is carried into the house, where the clean-lined surface of lower-level plaster is countered by the mortar-washed texture of the upper walls. The roof is supported by the seemingly endless exposed steel ridge bridging along small figural posts that stand down onto dividing cross walls, with the last of these a floating screen wall that conceals an east-facing window made to trap morning light above the kitchen.

Ultimately it is a project of layered oppositions – a linear structure in an amorphous site, a formal façade made of typical materials, plastic plaster surfaces versus expressive tectonic structure, trapped light on a dark foreground, and a steel beam that does not begin or end but lands along the way.

ダブリンの中心部にはジョージアン様式やヴィクトリア様式の建物が多く建ち並ぶが、その外側には、20世紀半ばに建てられた郊外型の一戸建て住宅が、連続住宅か二軒連続住宅のペアとして、ほぼ途切れることなく環状に並んでいる。これらの住宅地の建物は、コンクリート・ブロック、セメント漆喰、屋根瓦を用いて非常に手頃な価格で建てられている。そのほとんどにおいて外部空間は非常に限られているが、時折、袋小路がつくる幾何学という素敵な偶然から、角ばった大きな庭が見いだされることがある。クライアントはそのような秘密の庭の一つを手に入れた。このくさび形の庭は、車1台分の幅で道路に接し、奥行きは23mまで伸びている。プロジェクトは、小さな既存住宅をこのユニークな敷地と接続させながら2倍の大きさにすることであった。

結果、敷地を分断して細長いブロックをおくことで、2種類の庭が生まれた。ひとつは日陰にある小さな玄関スペースであり、もうひとつは、緑地、底上げ花壇、小さな果樹園のある日当たりのよい裏庭である。このランドスケープに対応するために形式的ファサードをデザインしたが、このランドスケープは滅多にないほど広い敷地を強調し、前後に並んだ窓が新しい大きなホール・ルームを通して2つの庭を繋いでいる。

住宅は近隣で一般的な素材を用いて建設された。よく見られる縮れた漆喰の下地と、小石を敷き詰めたようなペブルドッシュ表面で仕上げられており、下層の漆喰のくっきりとしたラインと、上方のモルタルで表面を仕上げたような壁の質感が対照的である。屋根は、仕切りとなる隔壁の上に立つ象徴的な小さな柱に沿って、無限に露出して見える鋼鉄製の部材で支えられている。最後にあるのが可動式のスクリーンウォールであり、キッチンの上に朝の光を閉じ込めるためにつくられた東向きの窓を隠している。

究極的には対立するものを重層化したプロジェクトであり、それをなすのは、無定形の敷地内の直線的構造体、典型的素材でつくられた形式的ファサード、可塑的な漆喰表面と表情豊かな建築構造の対立、ほの暗い前景に閉じこめられた光、始まりも終わりも無く途中で着地する鉄骨の梁などである。

（松本晴子訳）

p. 73: Ground-floor kitchen and dining. Photos on pp. 73–77 by Johan Dehlin.

73頁：地上階のキッチン・ダイニング。

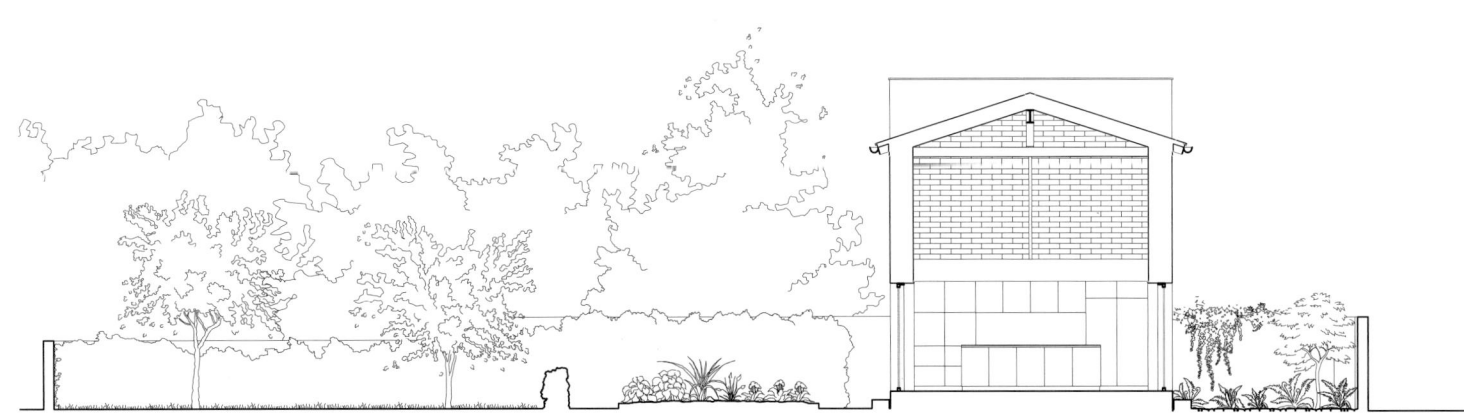

Section (scale: 1/150)／断面図（縮尺：1/150）

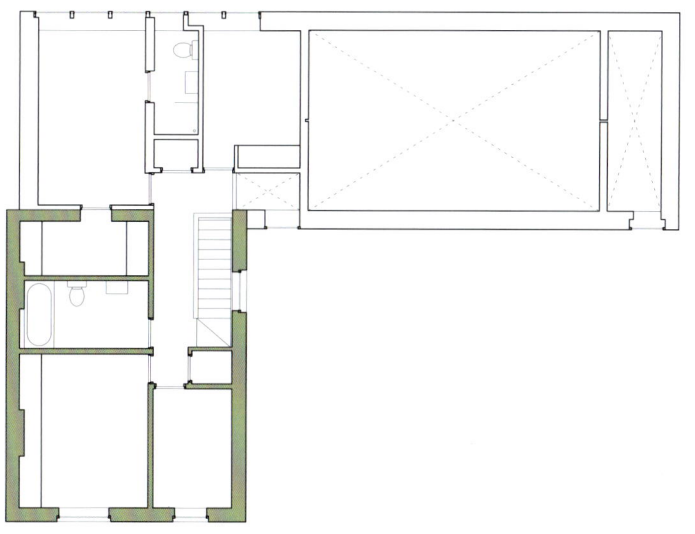

2nd-floor plan／2階平面図

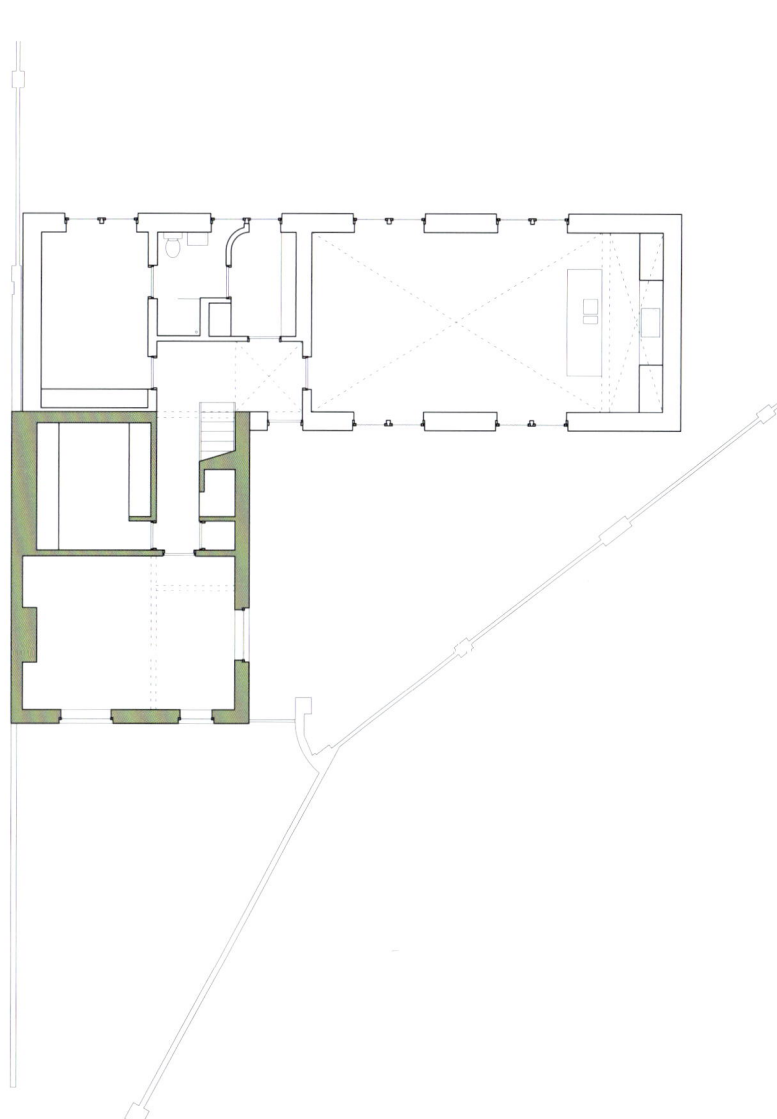

Ground-floor plan (scale: 1/200)／地上階平面図（縮尺：1/200）

Credits and Data
Project title: Dromlee House
Client: Private
Location: Dublin, Ireland
Design: 2020
Completion: 2022
Architect: Ryan W. Kennihan Architects
Design team: Ryan Kennihan, Emma Kavanagh, Jarek Adamczuk
Project team: BSG Homes (contractor), Brunner Consulting Engineers (engineering)
Site area: 684 m^2
Gross floor area: 207 m^2

p. 74: Beam detail. This page, top: West façade. This page, bottom: East façade with the roof of the addition visible on the right. Opposite: Detail of roof and façade.

74頁:梁のディテール。本頁、上:西側ファサード。本頁、下:東側ファサード、右奥に増築棟の屋根を見る。右頁:屋根とファサードのディテール。

Ryan W. Kennihan Architects
Baltrasna House
Dublin, Ireland 2017–2020

ライアン・W・ケニハン・アーキテクツ
バルトラスナ・ハウス
アイルランド、ダブリン 2017〜2020

The site for this house contained a ruined farmhouse and barns that had been in the client's family since the early 1800s. Its layout was typical of the vernacular farmhouse, with a series of simple pitched roof volumes arranged around several yards to provide shelter from the coastal weather. These buildings and yards accumulate incrementally over generations with new structures added to accommodate new uses.

The initial client brief was to renovate the existing buildings – but we enjoyed the buildings as ruins. In the missing cob and stone walls, in the broken windows and weathered shutters, in the cast-iron stove and stable hitches, in the egg boxes and broken books, we could see the lives of those who had lived there before and could feel the slow passage of time. To renovate would be to erase the mysterious joy of the ruin, so we decided to add to the complex of buildings in the historical way, by adding just a single, simple building. In the process we created a series of outdoor garden rooms within and between the existing buildings.

As the form and materials resonate with the surrounding buildings they make a house that is simultaneously old and new. Its construction is in simple block walls washed with mortar internally, and all the openings are glazed doors, allowing one to move freely between new rooms and garden rooms. The simple pitched roof externally conceals a variety of "tented" ceilings internally, which gives each room unique character and playfulness.

敷地には廃墟となった農家と納屋があり、1800年代初頭からクライアントの家族が所有してきた。土地に典型的な農家タイプの配置で、シンプルな勾配屋根のヴォリュームが芝地に配され、海岸沿いの天候からのシェルターとなる。建物と芝地は数世代にわたって少しずつ蓄積されており、新しい用途に対応するために随時構造が追加されていった。クライアントの当初の要望は既存建物を改修することであった。しかし、我々は廃墟を廃墟のまま楽しみたいと感じた。欠けた塊、石の壁、割れた窓、朽ちはてた雨戸、鋳鉄製のストーブ、馬小屋の馬をつなぐ杭、卵箱、壊れた本からは、ここに住んだ人々の生活が垣間見え、ゆっくりとした時の流れを感じることができる。住宅へと改築してしまえば廃墟の神秘的魅力は消えてしまうだろう。そこで我々は、過去にこの場所で行われてきたように、建物群にシンプルな建物をさらに一棟追加することとした。その過程で、既存建物の内部や建物同士の間に連続する屋外ガーデン・ルームをつくりだした。

形態と素材は周囲の建物と共鳴するよう選ばれ、古さと新しさを同時に感じさせる。内部はモルタル塗りのブロック塀でシンプルに構成され、開口部は全てガラス扉からなり、部屋とガーデン・ルームを自由に行き来できるようにつくられている。シンプルな勾配屋根の内部に様々な「テント」状の天井が隠されており、各部屋がユニークな個性と遊び心を備えている。
(松本晴子訳)

This page, bottom left: South façade. Photos on pp. 78–83 by Aisling McCoy. This page, bottom right: North façade. Opposite: Ruins run along the west side of the newly constructed house.

本頁、左下：南ファサード。本頁、右下：北ファサード。右頁：新築された住宅の西側に隣接する廃墟。

ARCHITECTURE AND URBANISM
24:03

642

Feature:
Irish Architecture
20 Houses by 6 Architects

Ryan W. Kennihan Architects
Baltraisna House
Dublin, Ireland

Credits and Data
Project title: Baltrasna House
Client: Private
Location: Dublin, Ireland
Design: 2017
Completion: 2020
Architect: Ryan W. Kennihan Architects
Design team: Ryan Kennihan, Jarek Adamczuk, Colin Mac Suibhne
Project team: Peter Taaffe Builder Ltd. (contractor), Ian Connolly – Downes Associates (engineering)
Site area: 1,085 m^2
Gross floor area: 274 m^2

pp. 80–81: West façade. p. 82: Corridor. p. 83: Living spaces in the north of the building.

80〜81頁：西側ファサード。82頁：廊下。83頁：北側に配された共有エリア。

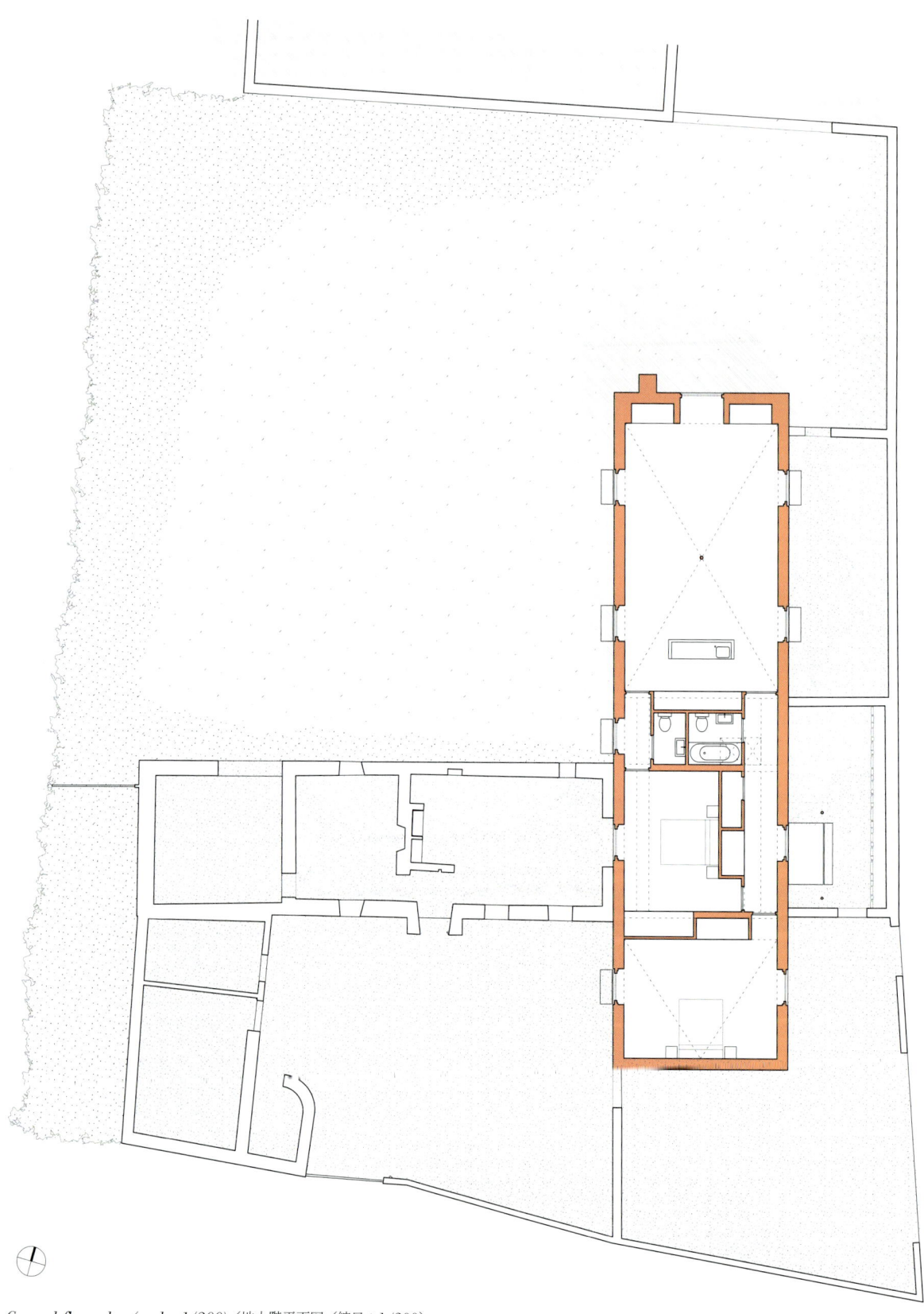

Ground-floor plan (scale: 1/200)／地上階平面図（縮尺：1/200）

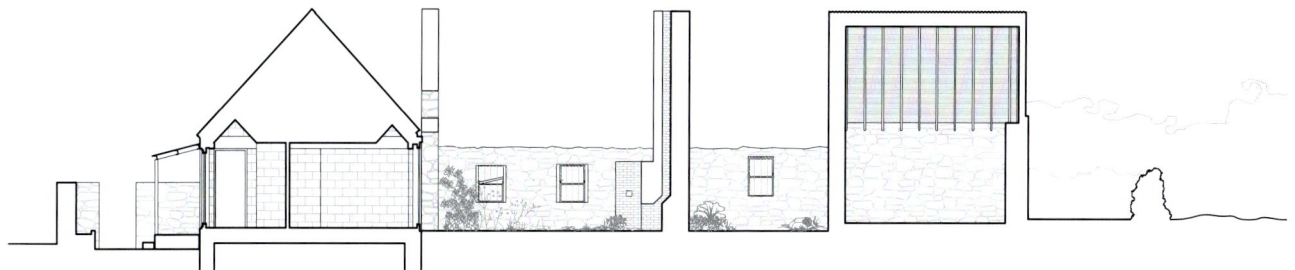

Transverse section／短手断面図

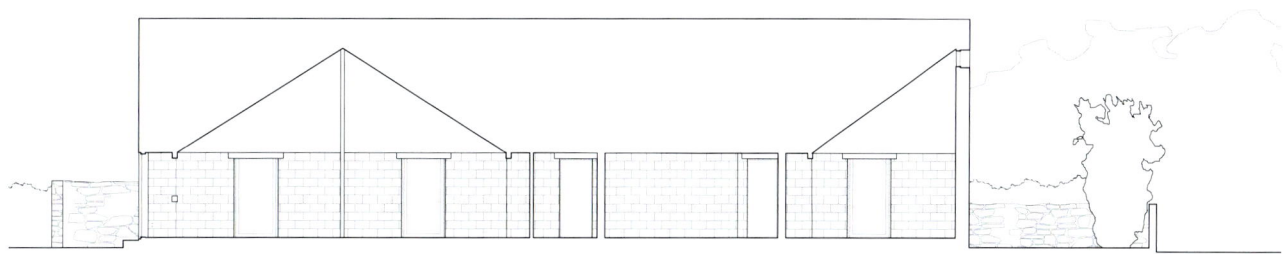

Longitudinal section (scale: 1/200)／長手断面図（縮尺：1/200）

West elevation (scale: 1/200)／西立面図（縮尺：1/200）

Ryan W. Kennihan Architects
Middle House
Dublin, Ireland 2020–2023

ライアン・W・ケニハン・アーキテクツ
ミドル・ハウス
アイルランド、ダブリン 2020〜2023

Our clients asked for a "meat and 2 veg" house – an Irish colloquialism for basic, standard, or no frills. They required a large but affordable house with 6 bedrooms and 7 bathrooms. Despite the momentum to move toward more sustainable methods, in Ireland, concrete-based construction continues to be significantly more economical than any other option. The formal and tectonic strategy for the house therefore evolved around the simple stacking of massive elements.
Externally the house is a collection of 3 volumes, each composed of 3 stacked layers. The façades of the house refer to formal tendencies found throughout the country in cultured houses of the "middle size," tending toward the simplicity of well-proportioned openings with a few subtle detail embellishments – here a slight step at the floors, there a slightly taller capping for an enigmatic asymmetry.
Meanwhile the tripartite layering also orders the interior, where lower walls of plaster rise to textured walls of painted block capped by hollow-core concrete spanning slabs, moving from more refined to more raw qualities. The need for the many rooms to connect to the perimeter walls left a spatial opportunity at the core of the house, where light from above washes down textured walls and leads one through the stepping section deep into the interior.
While the substance of the house is completely typical – standard block cavity walls, off-the-shelf precast lintels, cappings and sills, stock hollow core, basic plaster, and paint – its ordinary means do not necessarily lead to ordinary ends.

クライアントが求めていたのは、「肉と野菜2品」——アイルランドの口語でベーシック、スタンダード、飾り気のなさを意味する——の住宅であった。彼らが求めたのは、6つの寝室と7つのバスルームを備えた、広いが手頃な住宅であった。持続可能工法に移行する機運があるにもかかわらず、アイルランドではコンクリート基礎の建築が圧倒的に安価である状態が続いている。そのため、形式・構造的に、この住宅では巨大な要素をシンプルに積み重ねる戦略をとることとなった。
外から見ると3つのヴォリュームの集合体に見え、それぞれのヴォリュームは3つの積み重ねられたレイヤーで構成からなる。ファサードは、均整のとれた開口部のディテールにさりげない装飾が施され、シンプルさが追求された。全国的に見られる「中規模」の文化的住宅の形態を参照している。床にわずかな段差がつけられ、少しだけ高さのついた笠木が謎めいた非対称性を生みだしている。
3層構造が内部秩序となり、低い場所の漆喰壁は上にいくにつれてコンクリートの中空コアで覆われた塗装されたブロックの質感ある壁となり、洗練から生々しさへと質感が変化する。多くの部屋を外周の壁とつなげる必要があったため、住宅の核となる部分に空間的可能性が残され、そこでは、上からの光が質感ある壁に注ぎ込み、人は段差のある部分を通って内部空間へと深く入っていく。
規格品ブロックの空洞壁、既製品のプレキャスト・コンクリートのまぐさ、笠木と敷居、平凡な中空コアスラブや標準的な漆喰や塗料など、住宅を構成する物質は典型ばかりである。平凡な方法が必ずしも平凡な結果につながるとは限らない。　　　（松本晴子訳）

This page: The atrium seen from the 2nd-floor gallery. Photos on pp. 86–89 by Johan Dehlin. p. 88, top: Kitchen and dining area. p. 88, bottom left: Entrance hall. p. 88, bottom right: Staircase. p. 89, bottom: Front façade.

本頁：2階のギャラリーから吹き抜けを見る。88頁、上：地上階キッチン・ダイニング。88頁、左下：地上階エントランス・ホール。88頁、右下：階段。89頁、下：正面ファサード。

642

建築と都市
ARCHITECTURE AND URBANISM
24:03

Feature:
Irish Architecture
20 Houses by 6 Architects

Ryan W. Kennihan Architects
Middle House
Dublin, Ireland

Credits and Data
Project title: Middle House
Client: Private
Location: Dublin, Ireland
Design: 2020
Completion: 2023
Architect: Ryan W. Kennihan Architects
Design team: Ryan Kennihan, Oisín Jacob, Emma Kavanagh
Project team: Brookstar Construction (contractor), Brunner Consulting Engineers (engineering)
Site area: 950 m^2
Gross floor area: 332 m^2

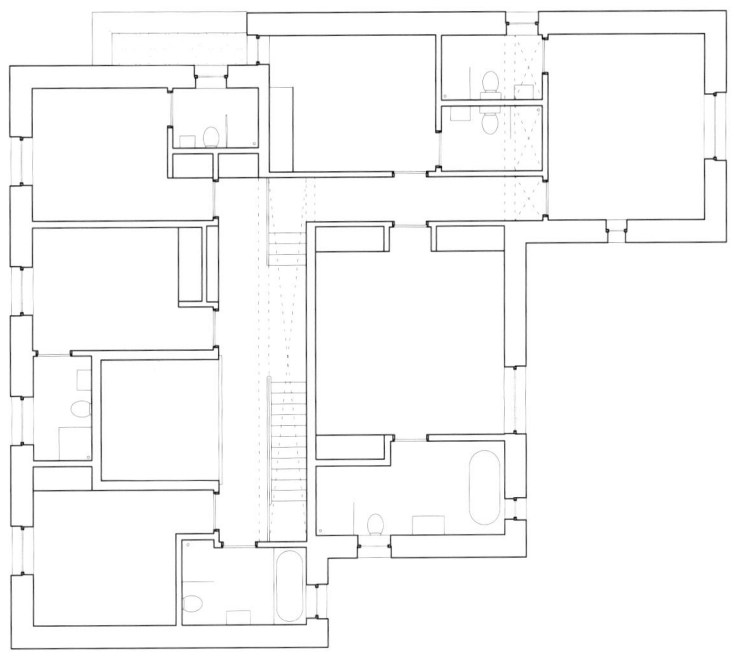

2nd-floor plan／2階平面図

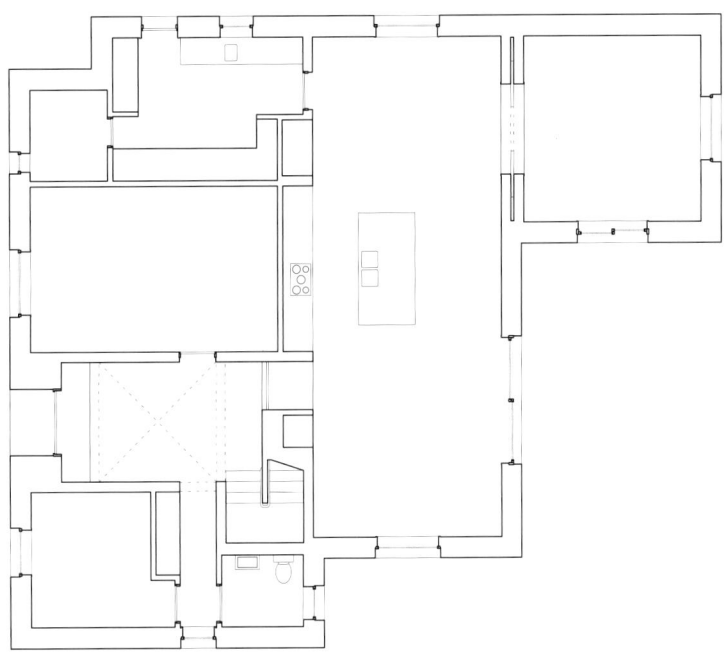

Ground-floor plan (scale: 1/180)／地上階平面図（縮尺：1/180）

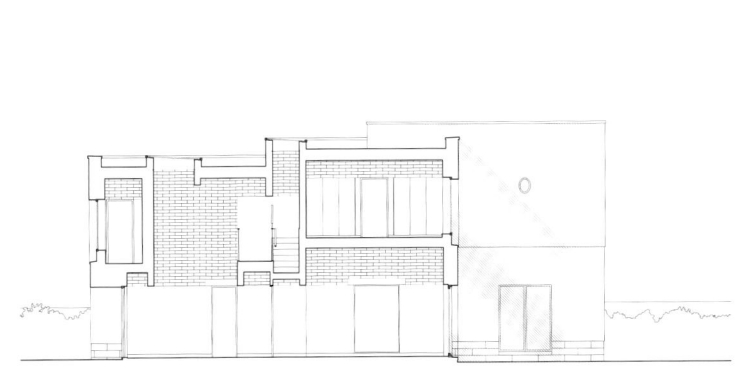

Section (scale: 1/250)／断面図（縮尺：1/250）

Ryan W. Kennihan Architects
Beach Road House
Galway, Ireland 2021

ライアン・W・ケニハン・アーキテクツ
ビーチ・ロード・ハウス
アイルランド、ゴールウェイ 2021

Connemara is a windswept, rough-hewn, and endlessly beautiful landscape. The commonly heard phrase "four seasons in a day" speaks to the ever-changing weather that can be both debilitating and invigorating. It also creates a perpetually changing and extraordinary display of light and color each day. Traveling west and leaving behind the town of Clifden, one arrives at the shores of the Atlantic, and the distinct feeling of being at the edge of the earth takes hold. "Here be dragons." In this sublime and tempestuous place, we have made a house that is both a sanctuary from and celebration of the elements. Wide overhanging eaves spread a feeling of shelter around the building, while robust concrete buttresses resist both the thrust of the roofs and the rush of the wind. Yet the structure is responsive to the weather. The buttresses hold the gutters down from the eaves to open a space for rain where one can see the rivulets fall from the corrugated steel. They also contain within them the downpipes, discharging the rain into 12 unique gullies so every turn of the rain is celebrated. The building resonates not only with vernacular form and material but also with the common post facto abutments found in many rural buildings. A slender and delicate internal structure serves as the counterpoint to the muscular external concrete. In the large hall there is play between this elegant tectonic and the abstract plane, between the curved form and the linear, between the repetitive and the singular. Bowed walls evoke the idea of sanctuary while making a space for dining and a space for preparing food.

コナマーラは風が吹き荒れる土地であり、荒削りで美しいランドスケープがどこまでも広がっている。「一日に四季がある」というフレーズをよく耳にするが、それは昔から変わらない天候を表しており、うんざりすることもあれば元気づけられることもある。また、四季は毎日絶え間なく移ろい、光と色彩が驚くような風景を生みだす。クリフデンの町を後にして西に向かっていくと、大西洋の岸辺に到着し、自分が地球の端部にいるのだという気持ちがはっきりとよぎる。「ここにはドラゴンがいる」
この崇高で昂るような場所において、我々がつくり上げたのは至聖所であり、諸元素にたいする賛美となる住宅である。大きく張りだした軒が建物の周囲へシェルターの感覚を広げている。頑丈なコンクリート製バットレスは屋根の突き上げにも突風にも耐える。とはいえ構造は天候に敏感に反応する。バットレスは軒先にぶら下がった雨樋を支え、雨水を集める空間を確保し、波板から細い水が流れ落ちる。また内部に雨樋が設置されており、12個の個性的な水路に雨水が排出され、循環する。この建物は、ヴァナキュラーなかたちと素材、そして多くの田舎の建物に見られるかつての迫持台と共鳴する。
細く繊細な内部構造は力強いコンクリート外壁と対をなす。大広間では、優美な構造と抽象的な平面、曲線と直線、反復と特異の間で相互作用が生じる。弓状の壁は至聖所を想起させ、食事の空間と料理の空間をなす。
この住宅に生命力が満ちるのは雨が降っているときであり、この「安全な港」を最も楽しめるのはまさにそのときである、というのが、住人たちの言葉である。

(松本晴子訳)

Opposite: Eave gutter detail. Photos on pp. 91–99 by Shantanu Starick. pp. 92–93: Aerial view of the 2 roofs. p. 94: West façade. p. 95: Opening in the east façade.

右頁：雨樋のディテール。92〜93頁：空撮、中庭を挟んで2つの屋根が並ぶ。94頁：西側ファサード。95頁：東側ファサードの開口。

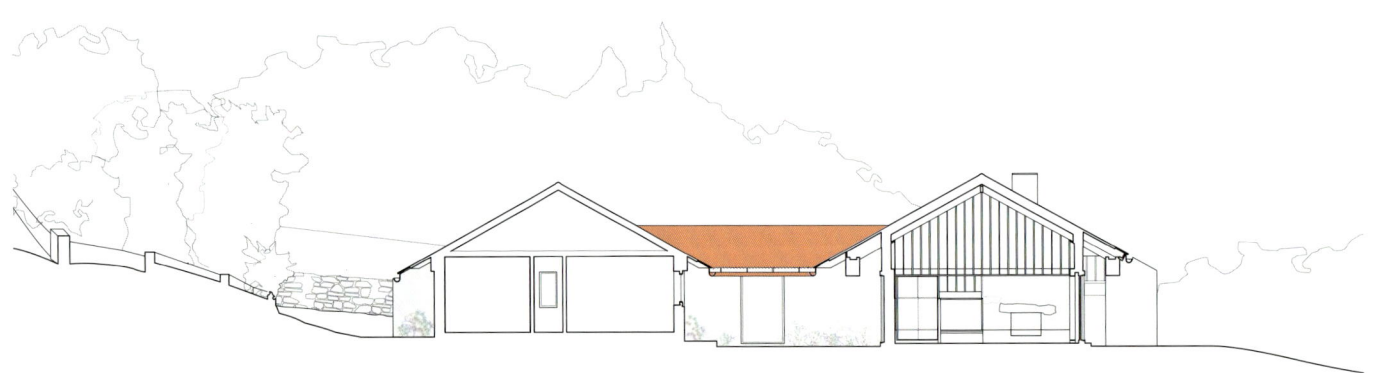

Section (scale: 1/200)／断面図（縮尺：1/200）

Credits and Data
Project title: Beach Road House
Client: Private
Location: Galway, Ireland
Completion: 2024
Architect: Ryan W. Kennihan Architects
Design team: Colm Macsuibhne, Jarek Adamczuk, Laura Carroll
Project team: Seán Burke Construction (contractor), Matthew O'Malley Timber (timber contractor), John Britton Consulting Engineers (engineering)

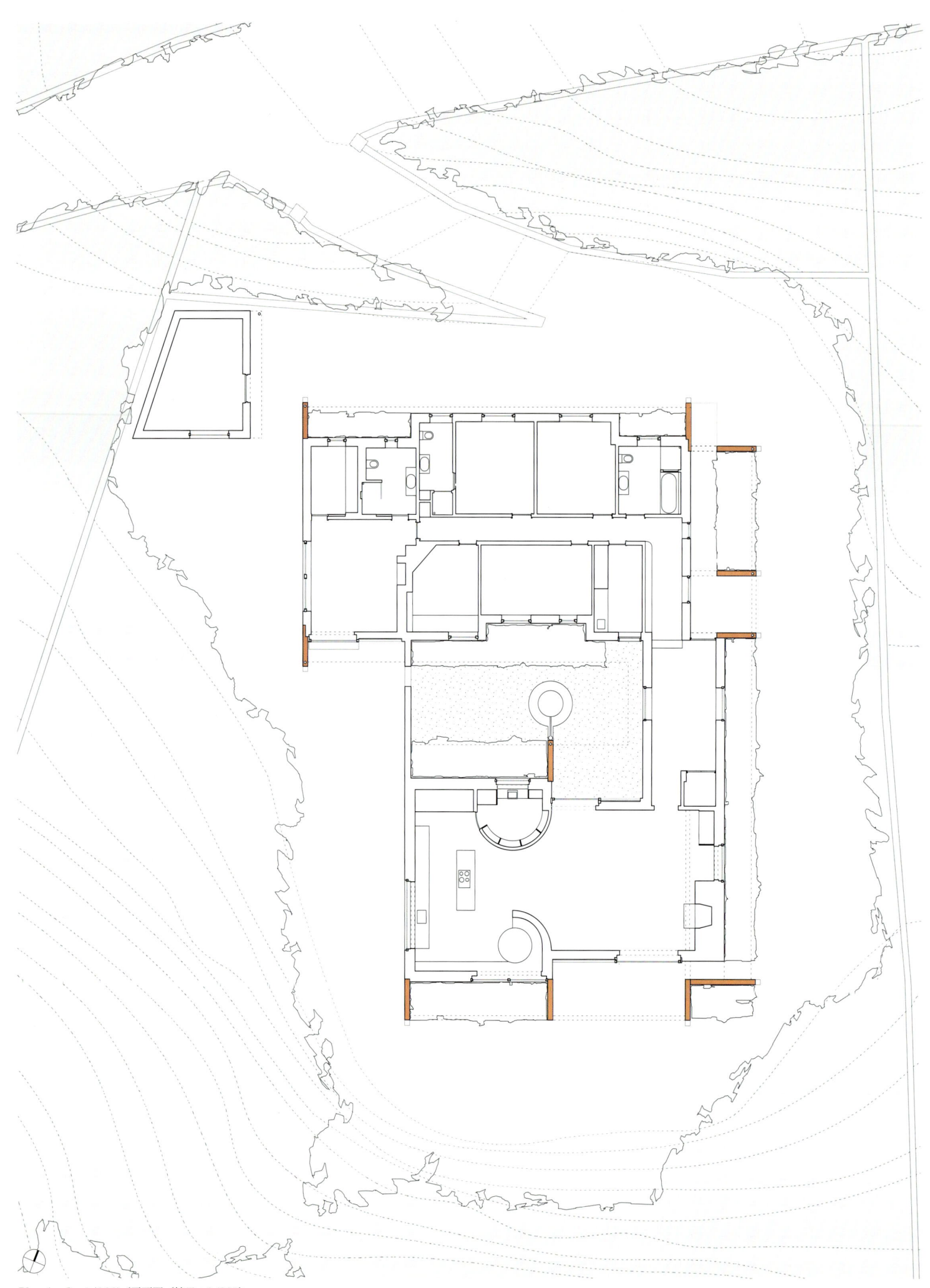

Plan (scale: 1/200)／平面図（縮尺：1/200）

pp. 96–97: The kitchen and dining space has built-in seating alcoves. This page: Dining space.

96〜97頁：キッチン・ダイニング、左に造付けのダイニング・スペースを見る。本頁：ダイニング・スペース。

From Inside to Out
内から外へ

Our projects often start with the detailed resolution of a specific experiential moment – where the layers of finish, structure, aperture, insulation, and weathering can be individually adapted to create a very specific condition: simultaneously experiential and instructive, fast and slow – revealing and heightening the layered nature of the enclosure. We find joy in the tailoring of these highly specific moments, searching for the personality of the whole.

TAKA architects

プロジェクトを開始するにあたって私たちはまず、人が経験する特定の場面の解像度を上げてゆく。こうしてレイヤーごとに、すなわち仕上げ、構造、開口、断熱、防水層ごとに調整を加えながら、まさに固有の状況を創出する。経験的にして教育的な場面、短くも長い場面によって、囲い（エンクロージャ）の重層性を浮き彫りにする。このように特定の場面をカスタマイズし、全体の個性を引きだしてゆくことに私たちは喜びを覚える。（土居純訳）

TAKAアーキテクツ

TAKA architects
Middleton Park Gate Lodge
Castletown Geoghegan, Ireland 2017–2020

TAKAアーキテクツ
ミドルトン・パーク・ゲート・ロッジ
アイルランド、カッスルタウン・ゲオギーガン　2017〜2020

建築と都市
ARCHITECTURE AND URBANISM
24:03

642

Feature:
Irish Architecture
20 Houses by 6 Architects

TAKA architects
Middleton Park Gate Lodge
Castletown Geoghegan, Ireland

This project involved extending 2 very small protected historic buildings – a gate lodge (to become a family home) and a kennel (to become guest accommodation) – both formerly part of the 19th-century Middleton Park House demesne.

The challenge seemed to be how to make new additions (both of which would be bigger in area than their corresponding original buildings) to these diminutive historic structures, without overwhelming them. We realized that if the new additions were partially sunk into the ground, then not only would their external bulk be diminished, but also new ways of experiencing the landscape from within would be possible.

We brought the external landscape right up to the internal living spaces – in the gate lodge at bench level, in the kennel at kitchen-counter level. At these moments we developed a deep threshold of overhanging roofs and wide sliding windows to allow generous openings to the outside, even when it rains. The new roofs have no gutters, which results in the rainwater flowing into a pond (by the guest house) or to the wildflower meadow.

2つの小さな歴史的保護建造物であるゲートロッジ（家族用の住居となる）と犬舎（ゲスト用の宿泊施設となる）の増築である。どちらの棟も19世紀につくられたミドルトン・パーク・ハウスの敷地にある。

課題となったのは、小ぶりな歴史的建造物を圧倒することなく、いかに増築部（どちらもオリジナルの建物より面積が広い）をつくるかであった。増築部を部分的に地中に埋め、外観の圧迫感を減らし、ランドスケープを内から体験することを可能にできると考えた。

ランドスケープは居住空間内部に入り込み、ゲートロッジはベンチの高さ、犬舎はキッチンカウンターの高さまで、ランドスケープに近づいている。このような場所に張りだした屋根、深い敷居、幅の広い引き違い窓を配置した。こうすることで雨が降っていても、屋外に大きく開く内部空間が可能となった。屋根には雨樋は設けず、雨水は池（ゲストハウス）や野草の生い茂る草地（家族用の住居）に導かれる。　　（松本晴子訳）

pp. 102–103: Exterior. Photos on pp. 102–111 by Alice Clancy. This page, top: Approach to the house. This page, middle: Entrance.

102〜103頁：外観。本頁、上：住宅へのアプローチ。本頁、下：エントランス。

Credits and Data
Project title: Middleton Park Gate Lodge
Client: Private
Location: Castletown Geoghegan, county Westmeath, Ireland
Design: 2017
Completion: 2020
Architect: TAKA architects
Design team: Cian Deegan (lead); Alice Casey, Bram D'hoedt, Ronan Lonergan
Project team: T&S McKeon (contractor), CORA (structure), Culligan Architects (conservation architect)
Site area: 3,200 m^2
Gross floor area: 149 m^2 (extensions), 81 m^2 (refurbishment)

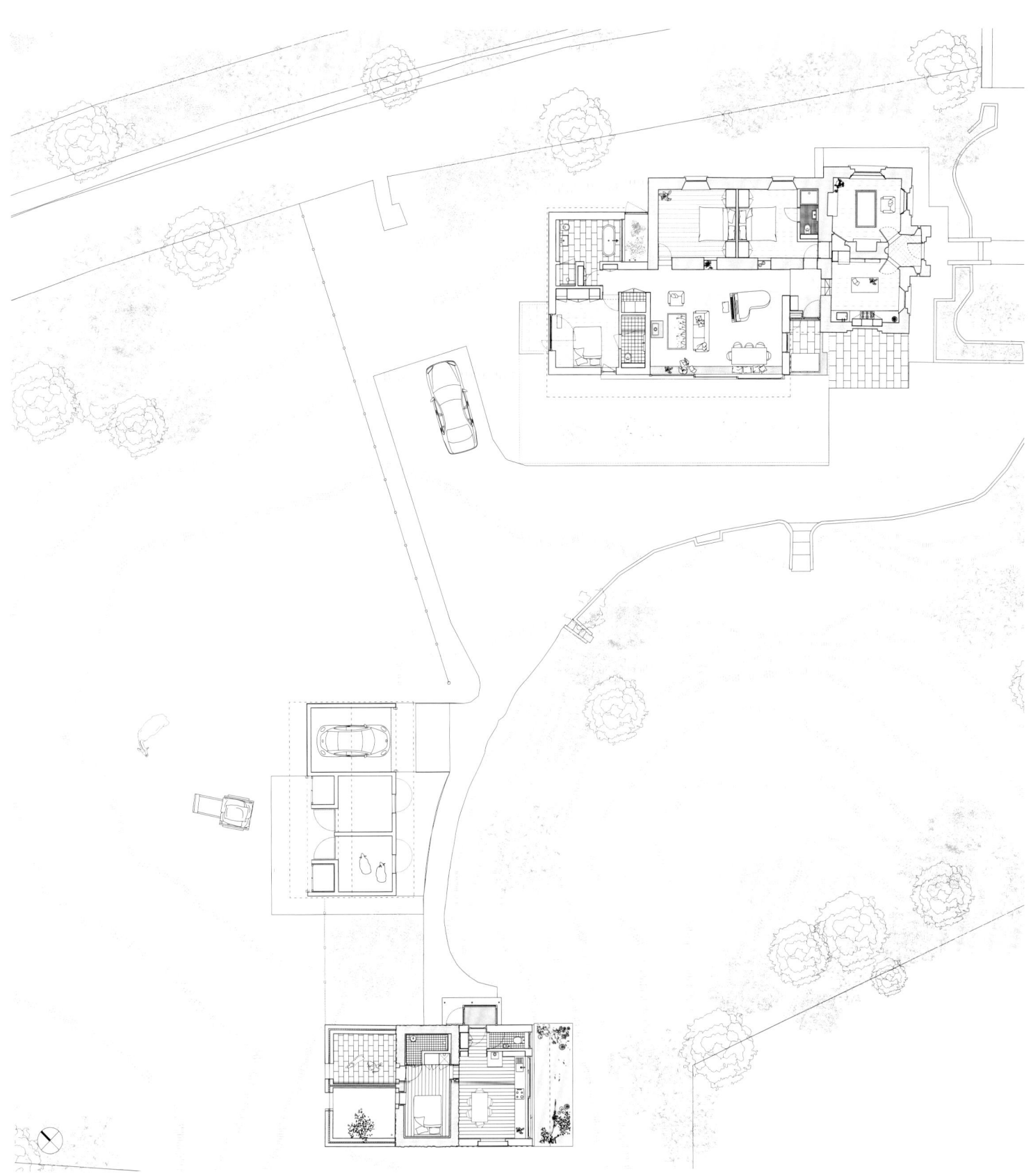

Site plan (scale: 1/300)／配置図（縮尺：1/300）

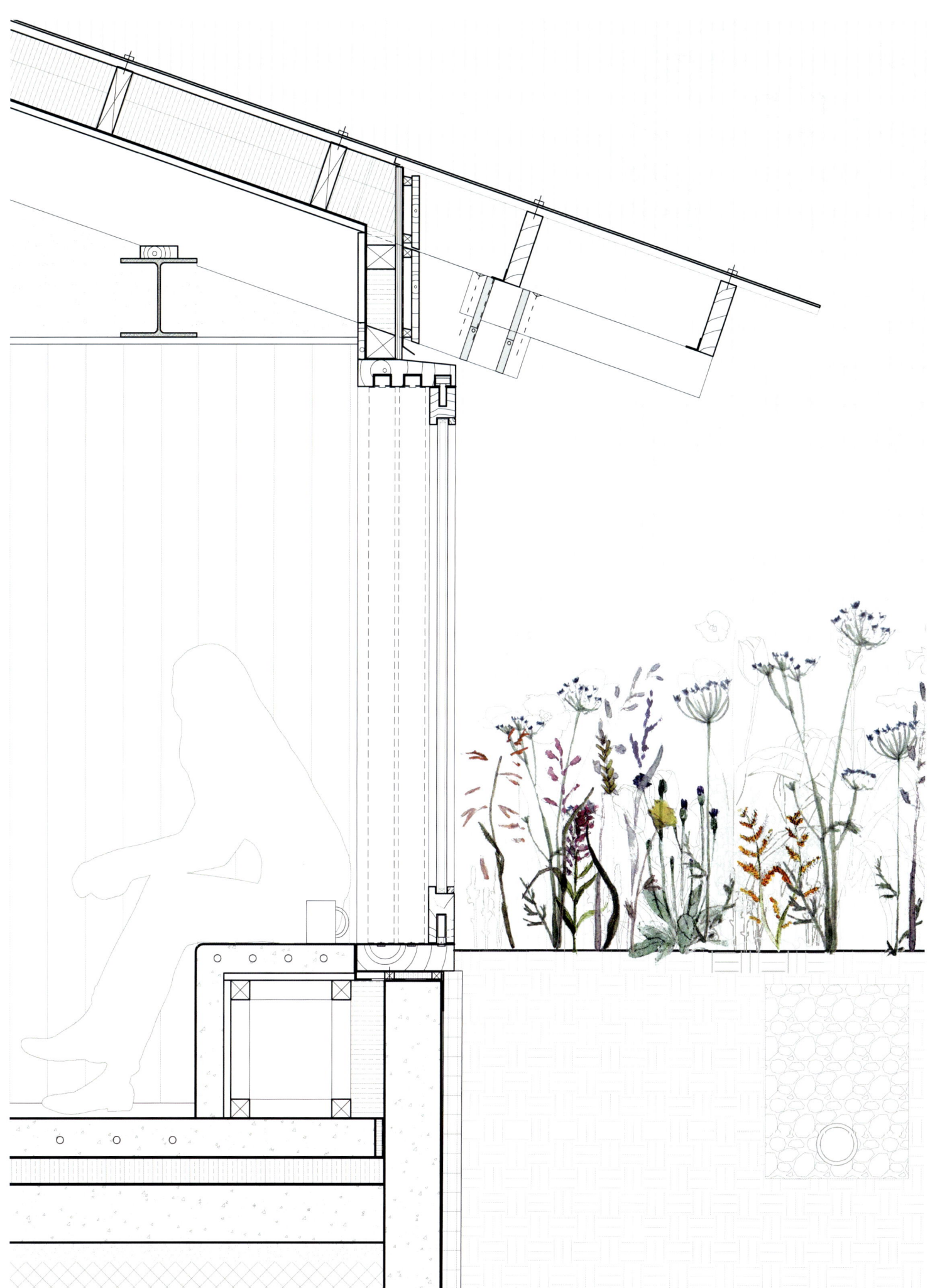

Detail section (scale: 1/15)／詳細断面図（縮尺：1/15）

p. 106: Sliding window with seating. pp. 108–109: Living area. This page, top: Study. This page, bottom: Kitchen. Opposite: Bedroom.

106頁：ソファのもうけられた引き窓。108〜109頁：居間エリア。本頁、上：書斎。本頁、下：キッチン。右頁：寝室。

TAKA architects
House 4
Dublin, Ireland 2010–2012

TAKAアーキテクツ
ハウス4
アイルランド、ダブリン　2010〜2012

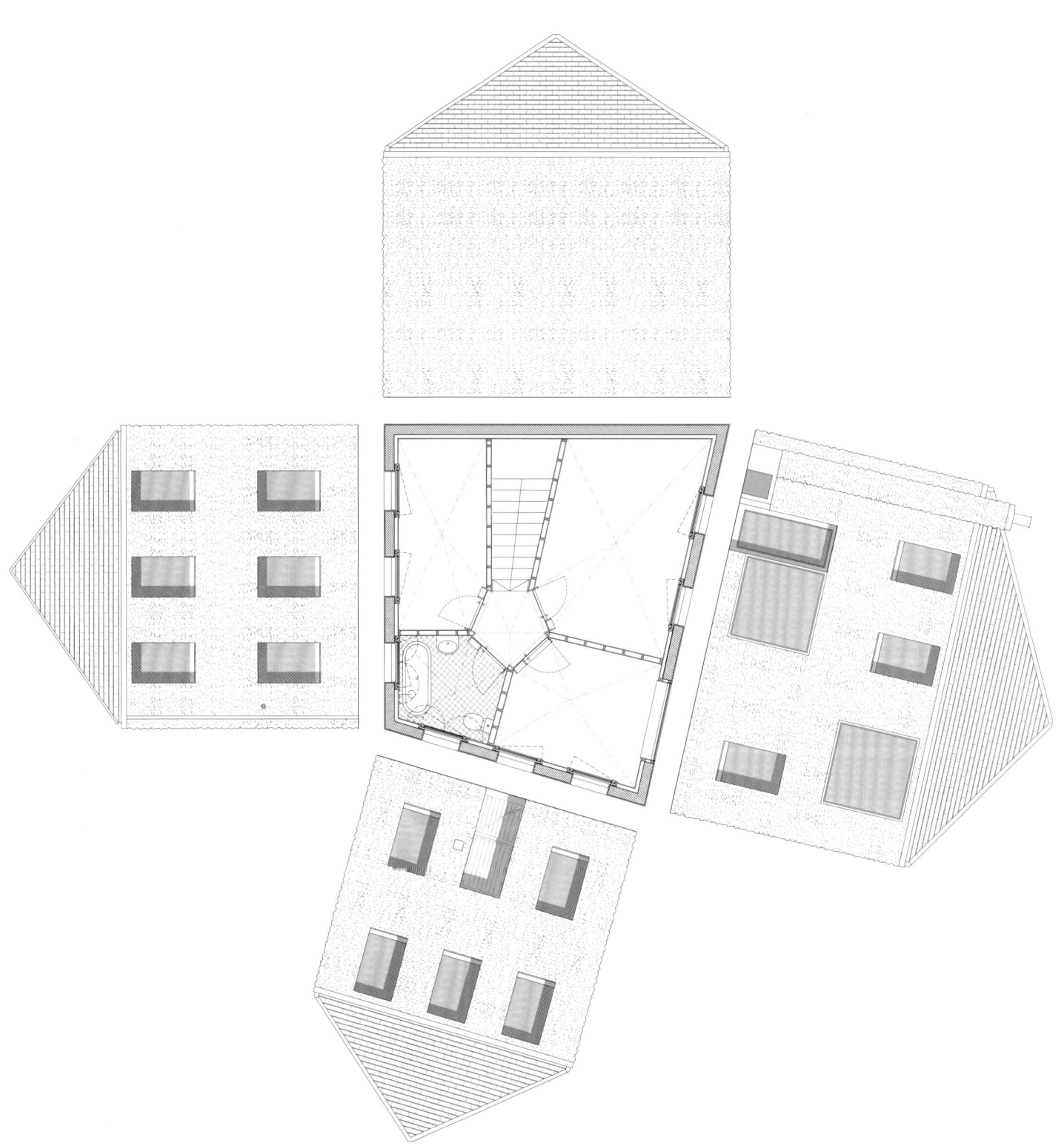

2nd-floor plan and elevations (scale: 1/125)／2階平面図、ファサード展開図（縮尺：1/125）

This is a small, newly built house on a leftover plot in a typical Dublin suburban housing estate. Its surrounding context is extremely coherent, as all the houses in the estate were built at the same time (late 1970s) and to the same design. We wanted this new house to be simultaneously similar to and different from its neighbors – like a granite boulder deposited by a glacier in an otherwise limestone landscape.

The external materials of the house are the same as those used for the neighboring suburban houses, with concrete roof tiles and pebbledash (small stones mixed with wet plaster) walls. But the details are different; the gutters are flush, while the pebbledash has larger aggregate and is left unpainted. The articulation of the windows became a focus for us – we were interested in them having a deep, raw presence, devoid of frame or sill.

Resolution of this window detail led us to a strategy of internally dry lining the structure with insulation with an additional lining of internal finishes. On the ground floor, birch-ply-fitted furniture lines the social spaces and houses storage and utilities. Upstairs in the private rooms, the lining is simple white plasterboard or tiles, with each room having an individually tented ceiling.

ダブリン郊外によくある住宅団地にある、余剰敷地に建てられた小住宅である。団地内の住宅はすべて同じ時期（1970年代後半）に建てられ、同じデザインの建物であるため、周辺状況は極めて似通っている。我々は近隣と似ているようで異なっている住宅をつくりたいと考えた――石灰岩のランドスケープにある、氷河によって堆積した花崗岩のように。

外壁材には、近隣の郊外住宅と同様に、コンクリート屋根瓦とペブルダッシュ（小石を湿った漆喰に混ぜた資材）を使用している。ディテールは異なっており、雨樋は水洗で、骨材の大きくペブルダッシュを用い、無塗装としている。焦点としたのは窓の減り張りであり、奥行きが深く、生々しい存在感をもち、窓枠や敷居がない窓を目指していた。

窓のディテールを解決することで、断熱材を施した構造内に乾いた裏地を施し、さらに内部仕上げに追加の裏地を施すという戦略にたどりついた。地上階の応接空間では、収納やユーティリティを収納するシラカバ合板の家具が裏地となる。2階の個室は、シンプルな白い石膏ボードやタイルを裏地とした。各部屋はテント状の天井に覆われる。

（松本晴子訳）

p. 113: Ground-floor window opening. Photos on pp. 113–114 by Alice Clancy. Opposite, top: Kitchen. Opposite bottom: Ground-floor fireplace.

113頁：地上階の開口。左頁、上：キッチン。左頁、下：地上階暖炉。

Credits and Data
Project title: House 4
Client: Private
Location: Firhouse, Dublin, Ireland
Design: 2010
Completion: 2012
Architect: TAKA architects
Design team: Cian Deegan (lead), Alice Casey
Project team: Sapele (contractor), CORA (structure)
Site area: 230 m²
Gross floor area: 90 m²

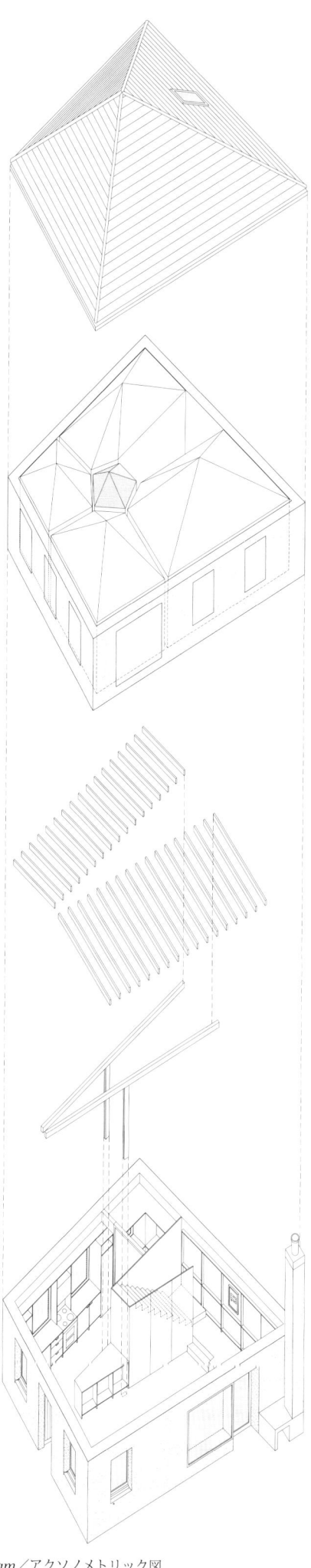

Axonometric diagram／アクソノメトリック図

TAKA architects
Brighton Road
Dublin, Ireland 2019–2021

TAKAアーキテクツ
ブライトン・ロード
アイルランド、ダブリン　2019〜2021

建築と都市 ARCHITECTURE AND URBANISM 24:03

642

Feature:
Irish Architecture
20 Houses by 6 Architects

TAKA architects
Brighton Road
Dublin, Ireland

p. 116: Entrance hall. Photos on pp. 116–120 by Aisling McCoy. p. 117: Dining area. This page: Clerestory window. Opposite: Exterior. p. 120: Plinth detail at the entrance.

116頁：エントランス・ホール。117頁：ダイニング・エリア。本頁：天窓。左頁：外観。120頁：エントランスの基壇ディテール。

This project is a refurbishment and extension of a protected historic building. While the original house is largely brought back to its original refined condition, for the addition we wanted to offer the family a different type of space – a domesticated cave, textural and atmospheric.

We began with an internally exposed concrete block-work structure, with the coursing of the block changing where light hits it directly.

The block-work window reveals are staggered in plan and section to give the impression of a raw archaic opening, which changes the atmosphere of the room. This constructional strategy (of exposed internal structure) leads to an external layer of insulation, which needs to be protected from the weather. We liked corrugated fiber-cement sheeting (something we had recently used as a roof material in another project). Using it here as vertical cladding, we expressed the sheet nature of the material by stepping out the cladding at the top of the elevation, revealing the thin corrugated edge profile.

歴史ある保護建築物の改修と増築である。オリジナルの住宅はほぼ元の洗練された状態に回復され、増築部には異なる空間、家庭化された洞窟のような、質感と雰囲気のある空間を考えた。

まず、内部に露出したコンクリート・ブロック構造から着手し、光が直接当たる部分でブロックの組み方が変化するようにした。

ブロック積みの開口部は、平面および断面上でずらして配置され、生々しく古めかしい開口という印象を与え、室内の雰囲気に変化をもたらしている。内部構造を露出させる戦略は外断熱層というアイディアにつながった。そのため外装を天候から保護する必要がでてきた。最近、別のプロジェクトで屋根材として使用した繊維セメント・シートを用いることとした。シートを垂直方向の被覆材として使用し、薄い波形板の端部の断面を露出、立面の最頂部の被覆材に段差をつけ、素材感を表現した。

(松本晴子訳)

Credits and Data
Project title: Brighton Road
Client: Private
Location: Rathgar, Dublin, Ireland
Design: 2019
Completion: 2021
Architect: TAKA architects
Design team: Alice Casey (lead); Cian Deegan, Bram D'hoedt, Jessica Keller
Project team: MDS Construction (contractor), CORA (structure), John McKinney (cost control), Culligan Architects (conservation architect), Acrewood (joinery)
Site area: 580 m^2
Gross floor area: 78 m^2 (extensions), 216 m^2 (refurbishment)

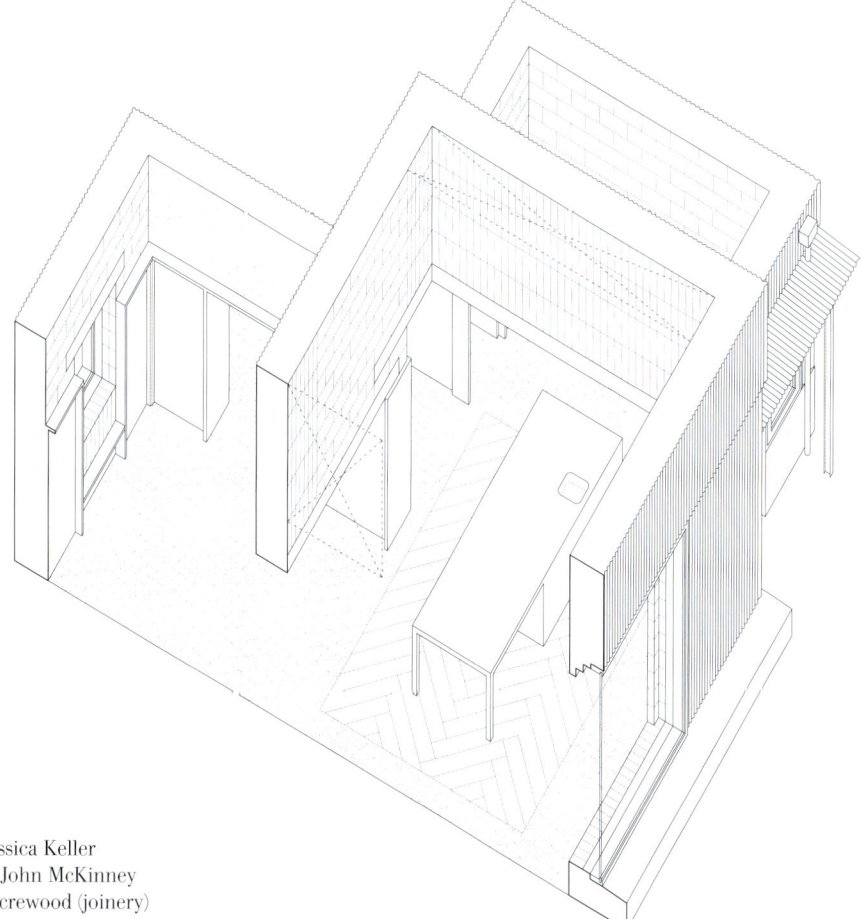

Axonometric diagram／アクソノメトリック図

Section (scale: 1/80)／断面図（縮尺：1/80）

TAKA architects
Reuben Street
Dublin, Ireland 2021–2022

TAKAアーキテクツ
ルーベン・ストリート
アイルランド、ダブリン 2021〜2022

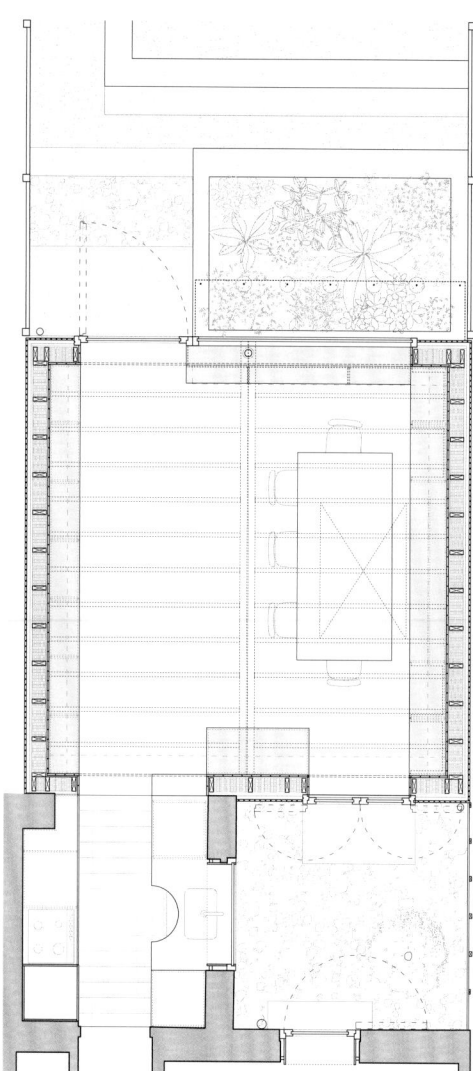

Ground-floor plan (scale: 1/80)／地上階平面図（縮尺：1/80）

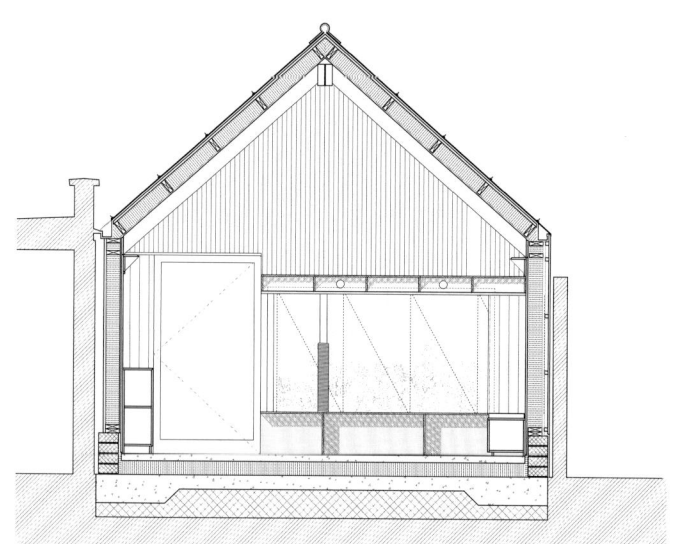

Section (scale: 1/80)／断面図（縮尺：1/80）

We designed this small single-room house addition for 2 visual artists. Early discussions with the clients focused on timber structures and the atmosphere in Japanese rooms and gardens. The structure is a simple symmetrical timber frame (albeit with a single steel column, which is revealed) with a pitched roof. A dark green stain on the interior timber cladding draws attention to the illuminated garden outside.

The large window to the rear garden has a low head height to pull the eye downward onto the outdoor planting, while outside the window, a low canopy subdues the direct light. Suspending the canopy from above and below using non-stretch yachting rope subtly weaves together the building and the garden.

2人のヴィジュアル・アーティストのため、小さなワンルーム住宅の建て増しを設計した。初期のクライアントとの話し合いで中心の話題となったのは、木造建築にすること、日本風の和室や庭園の雰囲気についてであった。

シンプルなシンメトリーの木造軸組（鉄骨の柱が1本だけ見えるが）からなり、屋根には勾配がついている。内部の木材は濃い緑色で塗られ、ライトアップされた屋外の庭園に視線を導いている。

裏庭に面した大きな窓は低めの頭上高に開けられ、視線をすぐ外側の植栽に集中させる。窓の外、低い位置にキャノピーがあり、直接光を抑制する。キャノピーは伸縮性のないヨット用ロープで上下から吊られている。こうして建物と庭園が絶妙に織り合わされている。　　　　　（松本晴子訳）

pp. 122: Exterior. Photos on pp. 122–125 by Aisling McCoy. p. 123: The eaves are fixed with yachting rope. Opposite: Living space.

122頁：外観。123頁：ヨットのロープで固定された軒。右頁：居間スペース。

Credits and Data
Project title: Reuben Street
Client: Private
Location: Rialto, Dublin, Ireland
Design: 2021
Completion: 2022
Architect: TAKA architects
Design team: Cian Deegan (lead); Alice Casey, Jessica Keller
Project team: The Red Lion (contractor), Brunner Consulting Engineers (structure), TTT thirtythreetrees (garden design)
Site area: 126 m^2
Gross floor area: 18 m^2 (extension)

Indeterminate Things

曖昧なもの

We layer our conversations with many small ideas, developing projects incrementally, positively reacting to constraints, building upon, or sometimes against, one another to form a whole. What comes before and after is often nonlinear. Like an architectural homophone, something can have duplicate reasonings or meanings – a pipe to distribute rainwater can shield a view or hold up a roof – an approach that can mean different things to different people. Discoveries are always judged experientially through scenography, be it model or drawing. Decisions are never made from abstractions, but instead from the experiences and the emotions they inflect.

David Leech Architects

私たちは、ちょっとしたアイディアを多数もち寄って会話を重ね、徐々にプロジェクトを練り上げ、そして各種制約を前向きに受けとめる。こうして個々の要素を積み上げ、時に相対立させながら全体を構成する。ただし、ある要素とその前後に来る要素とが一直線に並ぶことは稀だ。これは、建築における同音異義語とでもいおうか、ひとつの要素が二通りの論理ないし意味を帯びるためである。たとえば雨樋が視線を遮ることもあれば、屋根を支えることもあるように、同じものを見ても人によって受けとり方は異なる。新たな発見に気づくのは、遠近感をもって模型なり図面なりを経験した場合に限られる。私たちは、物事を決して抽象的な観念では判断せず、あくまで具体的な経験と、その経験から湧いた感情によって判断する。(土居純訳)

デイヴィッド・リーチ・アーキテクツ

David Leech Architects
House and a Garden
Dublin, Ireland 2007–2018

デイヴィッド・リーチ・アーキテクツ
家と庭
アイルランド、ダブリン　2007 〜 2018

This house is situated in a garden at the end of a short terrace of a 1940s estate on the edge of Dublin city – bounded to the south by a suburban hedge of hazel and privet, to the northwest by the blank wall of the original terrace, and to the northeast by a high wall backing onto a public laneway.

The ground-floor layout derives from the planning requirements for outdoor amenity space. To maximize the presence of the garden it takes advantage of the excellent privacy provided by the thick hedgerow. At the ground level all the supporting walls are located within an internal cross-shaped core, allowing a curtain of glass-and-timber folding doors to wrap the exterior of the house for direct connection and access to the garden. Internally, a cross-shaped core divides the plan into 4 public rooms: a hall/library, kitchen, dining room, and living room. These spaces are located according to proportion and orientation, and they step in section to accommodate ceiling heights of varying dimension and intimacy. A recessed ceiling track allows the rooms to be completely wrapped in woolen curtain like a medieval 4-poster bed. The core contains the service and plumbed elements of the plant, wash closet, kitchen appliances, and fireplace, as well as storage and the staircase. A loop of circulation runs continuously around the perimeter. On fine days, the folding doors can slide back from their corners allowing the house to spread outside, reducing the house's footprint to the structural core.

The gardens are planted to provide a variety of flora, much of it edible, responding to light, shade, aspect, and condition. A south-facing terrace includes a bench built into a new, inhabited garden wall.

The first floor is laid out with 3 bedrooms and a bathroom off a small central landing. Lit from a tall roof light contained within an extruded chimneystack, the landing is lined in timber paneling up to door height. The landing is the width of a single door and 2 doors in length. From this space, paneled doors open into generously proportioned bedrooms side lit from large windows sitting on the skirting of the opposing walls. The ceilings are draped along the pitch of the roof, falling from 4.5 m above the sweep of the doorway to 2 m around the perimeter. These rooms are clad in through-colored Valchromat MDF with a marquetry Valchromat MDF floor. Radiators, sockets, MVHR grilles, sensors, and switches are distributed within these MDF elaborations.

Externally, the house is treated in a manner similar but exaggerated to the immediate terrace housing. The masonry walls are finished in a pigmented off-white cementitious render, deeply roughcast on the garden side and hand-troweled smooth on the laneway elevation and public faces.

A heather-colored fiber cement roof has expressed untreated copper crampons, copper guttering, and tall standing seam hips. Copper downpipes draw figures across blank parts of the façade, reminiscent of a line drawing. Over time these elements will oxidize to a pale powder green.

Where the house meets the laneway a simple gable is projected with the image of a doorway and window set in relief.

pp. 128–129: West corner cantilever. Photo by Noel Bowler. Opposite: Street façade. Photos on pp. 130–131 by David Leech. This page: The back garden of the house.

128〜129頁：西側の角の開口部。左頁：通りからの外観。本頁：庭から住宅を見る。

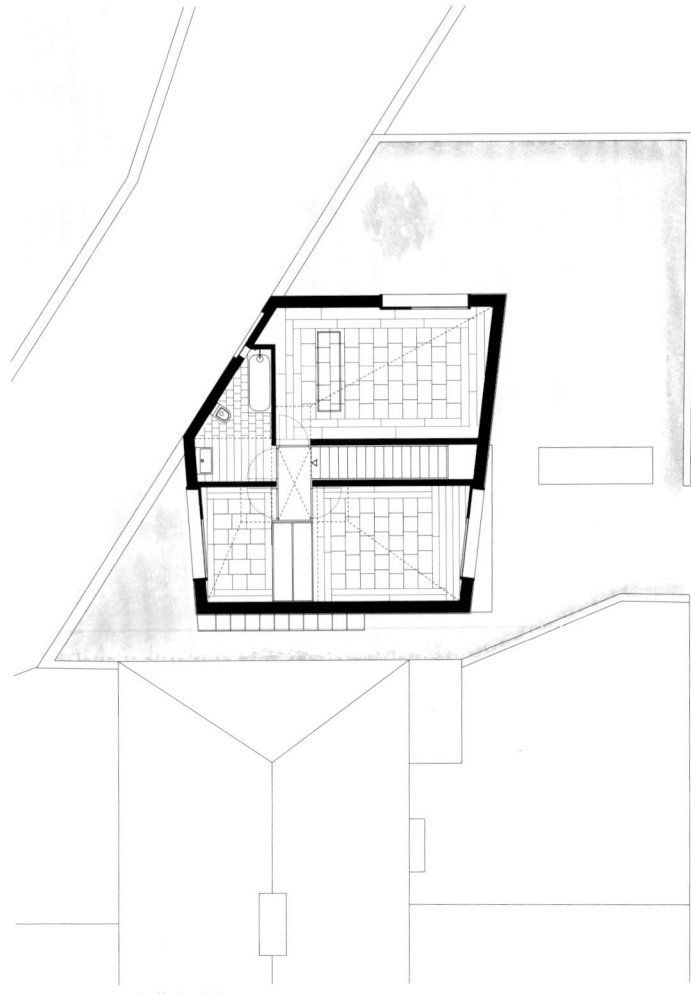

2nd-floor plan／2階平面図

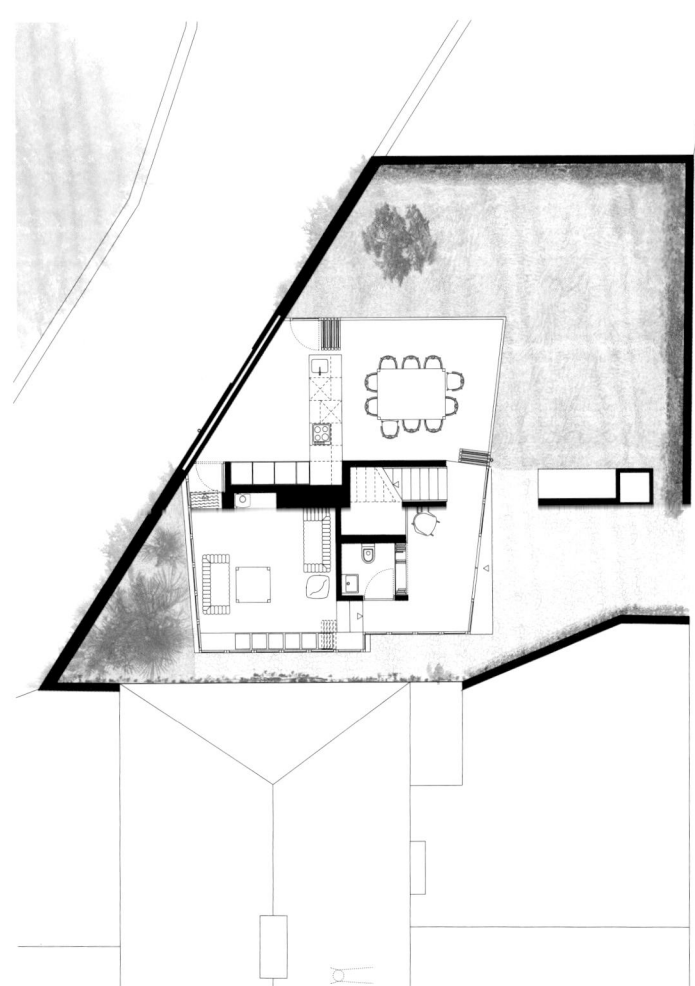

Ground-floor plan (scale: 1/200)／地上階平面図（縮尺：1/200）

この住宅は、ダブリン市街はずれ、1940年代につくられた地所にあり、幅の狭いテラスの端、庭の中にたつ。南側をハシバミとイボタノキの生垣、北西側を元々あるテラスの開口部のない壁、北東側を公道に面した高い壁で囲まれている。

地上階の平面配置は、屋外のアメニティ空間の計画要件から導きだされた。庭を最大限に生かすため、太い生垣によってプライヴァシーが確保された。地上階レヴェルにおいて、すべての壁は十字型コアの中に配され、ガラスと木製の折り畳み式扉によって庭に直接アクセスできる。

十字型コアが、内部をホール／図書室、キッチン、ダイニング、リヴィング・ルームと4つのパブリック・ルームに分割する。これら部屋は比率と方角に従って配置され、断面に段差をつけることでできた多様な天井高が、多様な性格の部屋をつくりだす。天井に埋め込まれたレールに毛織物のカーテンをとりつけることで、部屋は中世の四柱式ベッドのようにすっぽりと包まれる。コアには、機械設備、洗面台、台所用品、暖炉、収納、階段などのサーヴィス要素や配管が隠される。動線は住宅の外周沿いに連続する。

天気の良い日には、折り畳み式扉を角まで引き込み、住宅を屋外まで拡張できる。この際住宅のフットプリントにあたるはコアのみとなる。

庭には食用の植物が多く植えられており、光、日陰、側面、条件に対応する。新たに設置された塀に囲まれている南向きのテラスにはベンチが設けた。

2階には、中央に小さな踊り場、それをはさんで3つの寝室と浴室がある。踊り場では、押しだし成形された煙突中にある高い天窓から採光がとられ、木製パネルが扉の高さまで壁を覆う。踊り場は、扉の幅1枚分と扉2枚分の長さがある。このスペースからパネル張りの扉を開けると、ゆったりとした寝室があり、反対側の壁の巾木に開けられた大きな窓から光が入る。天井は屋根勾配に沿って垂れ下がり、出入口の掃きだしの上では4.5mあった天高が外側では2mとなる。寝室の床は、寄木のヴァルクロマットMDFパネルで敷きつめられ、貫通色のヴァルクロマットMDFパネルと組み合わされている。ラジエーター、ソケット、MHVRグリル、センサー、スイッチ類は、これらのMDFの中にはめこまれている。

この住宅の外観は、すぐ隣のテラスハウスに大げさなまでに似せている。石積みの壁は顔料を混ぜたオフホワイトのセメント系塗料で仕上げられた。庭側では濃く荒塗りされ、車道側と公道側は手鏝で滑らかに仕上げられている。

青紫色の繊維セメント屋根は、未加工の銅製の鋲、銅製の雨樋、背の高いスタンディング・シームの隅棟を備え、精巧に仕上げられている。銅製の雨樋は、線のようにファサードの空白部分に図形を描く。時間の経過とともにこれら要素は酸化し、淡いパウダーグリーンに変化していくだろう。

住宅と車道が接する部分には、出入口と窓のイメージを浮き彫りにしたシンプルな切妻が投影されている。　　（松本晴子訳）

p. 134: Primary bedroom. Photos on pp. 134–135 by David Grandorge. p. 135: Living room.

134頁：2階の主寝室。135頁：北側の中庭に面した居間。

Credits and Data
Project title: House and a Garden
Client: Private
Location: Dublin, Ireland
Design: 2007
Completion: 2018
Architect: David Leech Architects
Design team: David Leech
Project team: CORA (structure)
Site area: 100 m²
Gross floor area: 120 m²

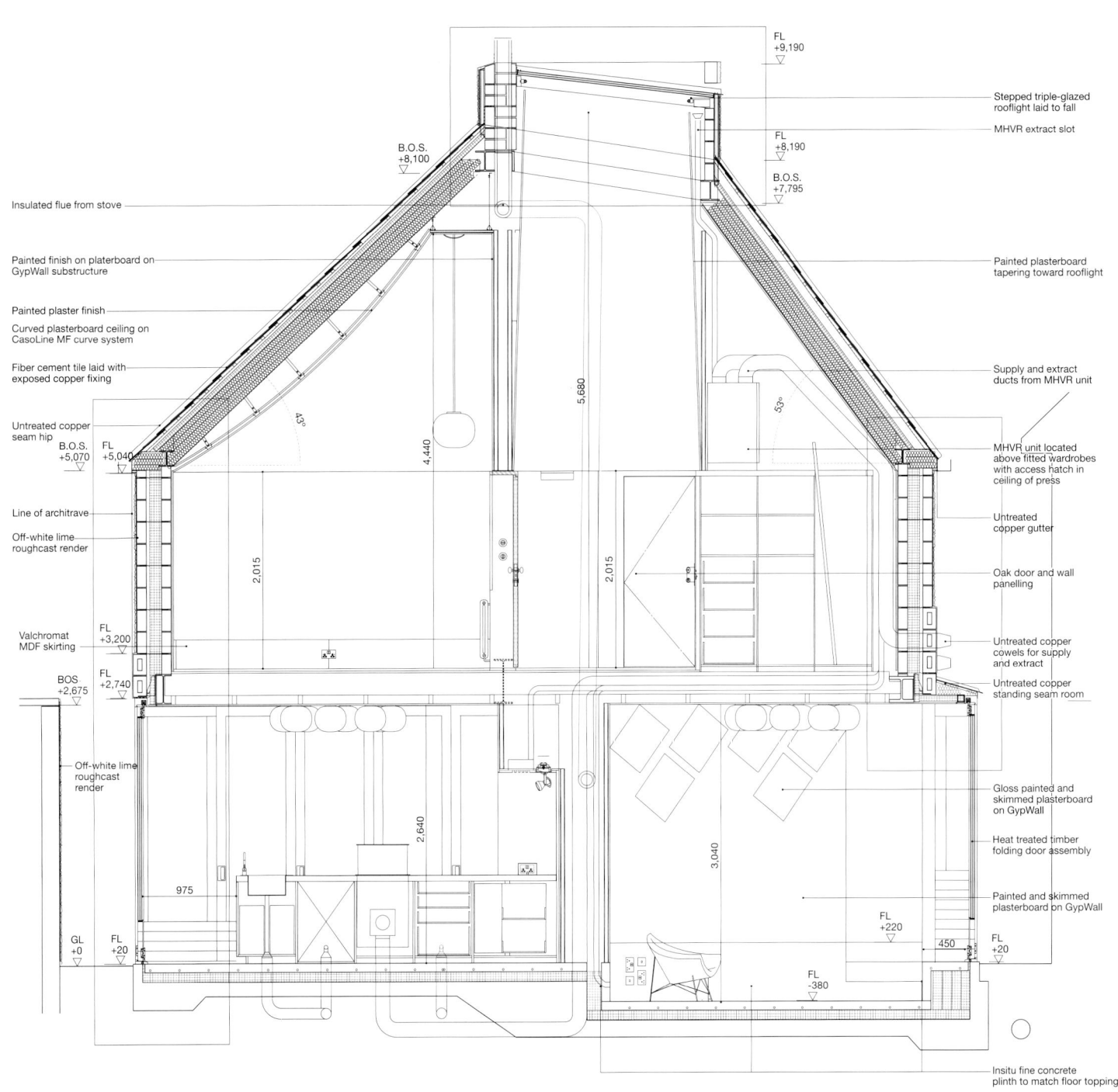

Detail section (scale: 1/60)／詳細断面図（縮尺：1/60）

David Leech Architects
Conservatory Room
Dublin, Ireland 2018–2019

デイヴィッド・リーチ・アーキテクツ
温室
アイルランド、ダブリン　2018〜2019

The character of this modest garden addition derives from the expression of a simple structural construction.
Standard timber joists, at 600 mm spacings, cross in both directions to allow for a free span between 2 rendered cavity walls. The timber beams sit on shallow pilasters formed where the block work is turned through 90 degrees to provide lateral restraint and to give a subtle relief to the bearing walls.
Above, slightly exposed beams create a shallow coffer; although contemporary in appearance, the filigree relief recalls Victorian orangeries and traditional conservatories. One large and 3 smaller proprietary roof lights form a loose constellation between the coffers and dictate the module. The roof lights are positioned so that a patterning of light moves across the wall over the course of a day as a 2nd order to the architecture. Another pattern of circular ceiling-mounted light fixtures form another order, which becomes more visible at night.
Color and polychromy are used as a way to mute the surface articulation of the ceiling and express the separate order of the roof lights to add richness, depth, and atmosphere.
The original window opening to the back room is enlarged to create a generous connection between a new kitchen and a new family room. A counter and cupboards are constructed with green through-colored Valchromat MDF accented by a polished marble countertop.
A small carpet of polished marble tiles embedded in a struck in situ concrete floor, left unpolished, conceals the drainage access. The rug of stone suggests inhabitation and aggregate – a contemporary translation of a Palladian terrazzo.
Plant and utility spaces are in an outhouse in the garden, which has a wall connecting it back to the main house. While the rhythm of the pilasters is continued along this edge, the wall between drops acknowledges the lower boundary condition. The pilasters extend beyond the wall to form 5 exposed columns, and this extended wall frames a new garden court with the columns protruding to hold the cross joisted ceiling structure, which is now fully exposed and forms a new open pergola hung with wisteria to provide shelter and shade.

この控えめな庭の増築はシンプルな構造体表現によって特徴づけられる。
標準材の木梁を600mm間隔で縦横に交差させ、2つの角材を組み合わせた中空壁間にフリースパンが生まれる。木梁は、角材を組み合わせた部位を90度回転させてつくられた奥行きの浅い付柱の上に設置され、横方向に制限をもたらし、耐力壁にできた繊細な浮き彫りとなる。
上部の梁はわずかに露出され奥行きの浅い格間をつくりだす。現代的な外観でありながらも、線条細工の模様のレリーフはヴィクトリア朝のオレンジ温室や伝統的な貯蔵所を彷彿させる。大きな天窓と小さな天窓3つが、格天井の間で緩やかな星座となり、モジュールを決定する。天窓は、第2の秩序となり、一日の間に光のパターンが壁を横切り移動するよう配置された。天井の円形照明器具からも光のパターンが生まれ、別の秩序を形成しており、夜になるとそちらがはっきりとしてくる。
多彩色が天井表面の接合部をぼかし、天窓のいくつかの秩序を表現する方法として使われ、豊かさや深みや雰囲気を空間に与える。
奥の部屋につながる開口部は、オリジナルの窓を拡張し、新しいキッチンと新しい家族室をつなぐゆとりある空間とされた。カウンターと食器棚はグリーンのヴァルクロマットMDFパネルでつくられ、研磨大理石のカウンタートップがアクセントとなる。

排水口は研磨大理石タイルの小さなカーペットで隠され、研磨していない現場打ちコンクリート床に埋め込まれた。大理石の絨毯は居住と集合体を暗示し、パッラーディオ様式のテラゾ（人造大理石）を現代風に解釈する。
設備用空間は庭の離れに設置された。この部屋と母屋は1枚の壁でつながっている。付柱のリズムはこの縁に沿って続き、下の壁が敷地境界を示す。付柱はその壁を越えて伸び、剥きだしの5本の柱として立っている。この拡張された壁から突きでた柱が新しい庭園広場を枠取り、ここでは完全に露天となった交差梁天井を支える。天井はフジが巻きつく開放的なパーゴラとなり、日除けと木陰をもたらしている。　（松本晴子訳）

Opposite: The garden addition has a polychromatic lattice ceiling. Photos on pp. 137, 140 by Jim Stephenson. p. 138: The family room with the garden addition. Photos on pp. 138–139 by Joseph Carr. p. 139: The lattice ceiling extends from the interior to the exterior. p. 140: Detail of the wall and ceiling.

右頁：格子天井に覆われたガーデン・ルーム。138頁：ファミリー・ルームと庭の接続。139頁：中から外に続く天井。140頁：壁と天井のディテール。

Credits and Data
Project title: Conservatory Room
Client: Private
Location: Dublin, Ireland
Design: 2018
Completion: 2019
Architect: David Leech Architects
Design team: David Leech
Project team: Ivan Cooney (structure)
Gross floor area: 25 m²

642

Feature:
Irish Architecture
20 Houses by 6 Architects

David Leech Architects
Conservatory Room
Dublin, Ireland

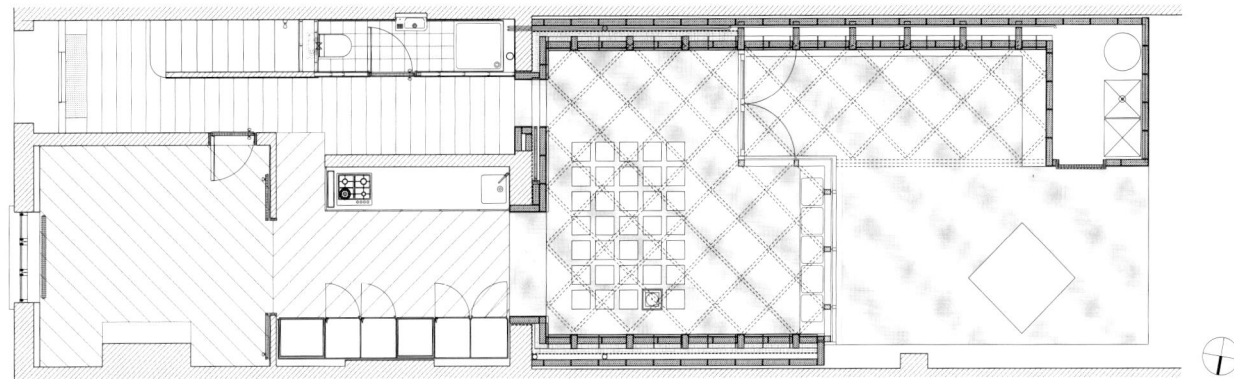

Plan (scale: 1/120)／平面図（縮尺：1/120）

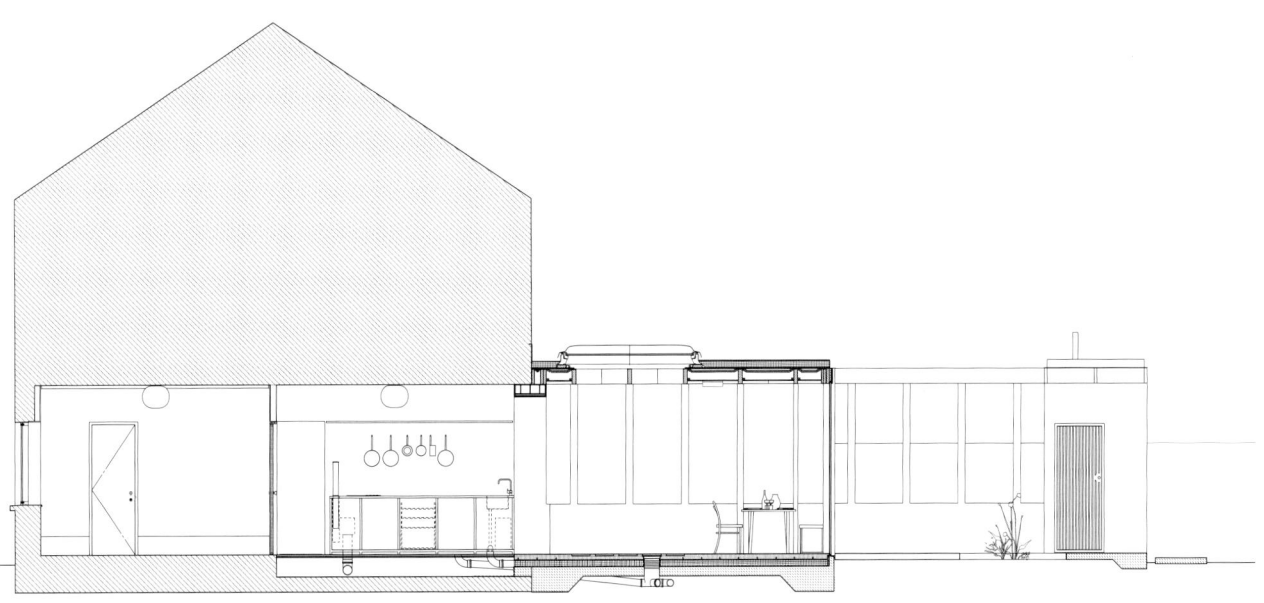

Section (scale: 1/120)／断面図（縮尺：1/120）

Between Thought and Feeling

思考と感情のはざまで

One day the monks of Clonmacnoise were holding a meeting on the floor of the church, and as they were at their deliberations there they saw a ship sailing over them in the air, going as it were on the sea. When the crew of the ship saw the meeting and the inhabited space below them, they dropped anchor, and the anchor came right down onto the floor of the church, and the priest seized it. A man came down out of the ship after the anchor, and he was swimming as if he were in the water, till he reached the anchor; and they were dragging him down then. "For God's Sake let me go!" said he, "for you are drowning me." Then he left them, swimming in the air as before, taking his anchor with him.[1]

This text is a loose assemblage of parts, made and then remade by multiple retellings, rewritings, translations over long periods of time, until it appears finally as a sort of absurd aphorism. It is a blunt ad hoc composition that lacks a narrative order such as a beginning, a middle, and an end: there is no embellishment; it is not resolved; it is odd and humorous. These compositional qualities draw one in, erasing the false distinction between thought and feeling – so it is with architecture.

t o b Architect

ある日、クロンマクノイズの修道士たちが教会の床に車座になって会合を開いていた。一座が真剣に協議していたその時、頭上に一隻の船が現れ、さながら海を航行するかのごとく宙を横切っていった。船の乗組員らは、この一座のいる空間を眼下に認めるや、錨を降ろし始めた。と、錨が教会の床めがけて落ちてきたので、司祭がこれをむずと掴んだ。錨に続いて男が一人、船を降り、まるで水を掻くようにして錨に向かって泳いできた。と、修道士たちが男を引きずり下ろした。「なんてこった、離してくれ!」と男。「俺を溺れさせる気か」と言い捨てるや、錨を抱えてまた宙を泳いでいった。[1]

以上は、部分を寄せ集めただけの散漫な文章である。いったんつくられた文章が、幾度も語り直され、書き直され、翻訳されるうちにつくり変えられ、ついには荒唐無稽なアフォリズムめいたものになっている。いわば成り行き任せの雑な作文にすぎず、起承転結の流れもなければ、修飾も落ちもない珍妙な文章だ。ところがその独特の味わいが読み手を引き込み、思考と感情との、ありもしない区別を無効にする。建築も然り。(土居純訳)

t o b アーキテクト

Note:
1. John Carey, *Aeriel Ships and Underwater Monasteries: The Evolution of a Monastic Marvel*, vol. 12 (Cambridge, MA: Harvard University, 1992), pp. 16–28.

原註:
1. 英文参照

t o b Architect
Killan Farmhouse
Bailieborough, Ireland 2015–2018

t o b アーキテクト
キラン・ファームハウス
アイルランド、ベイリーバラ　2015〜2018

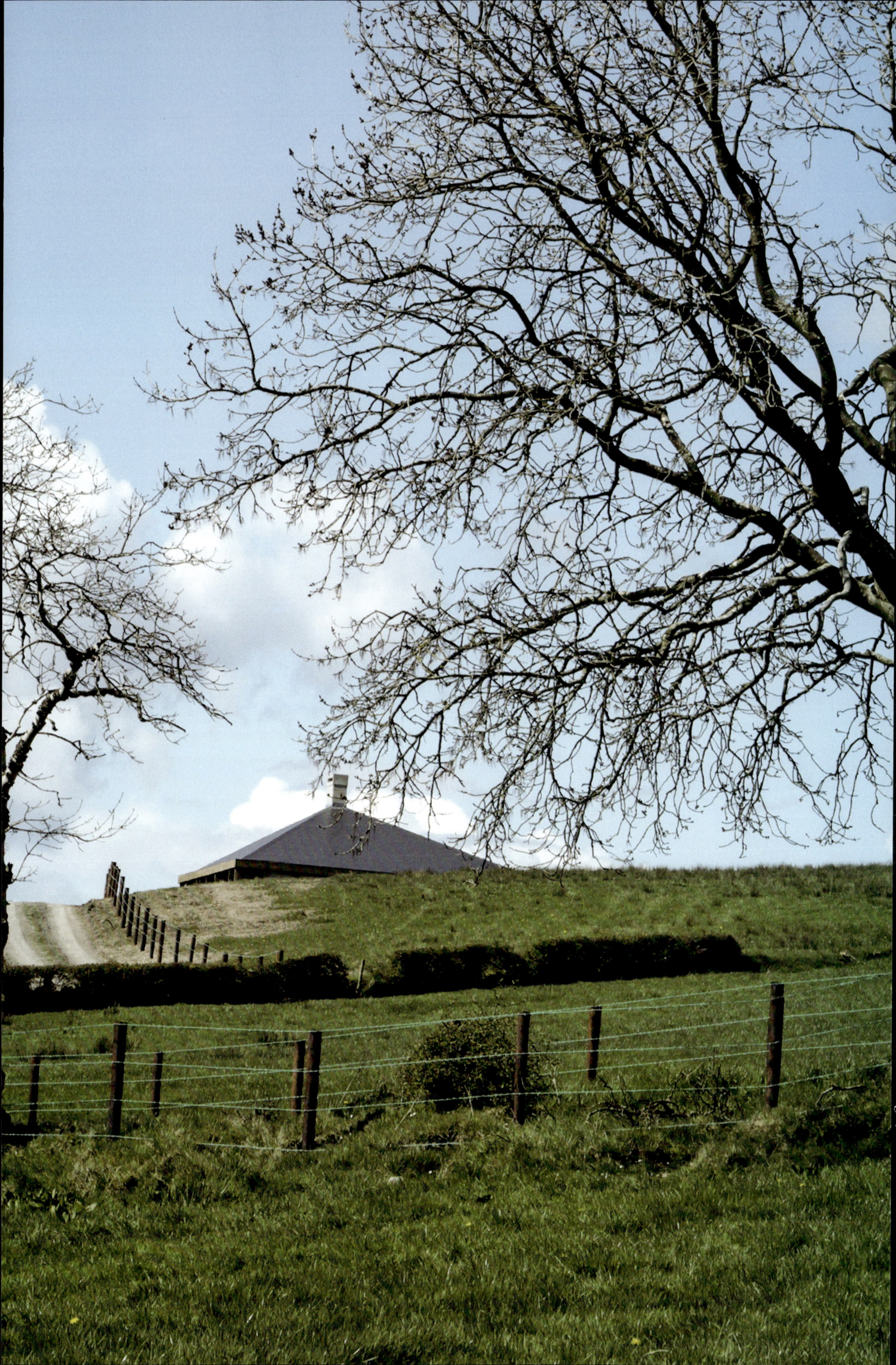

建築と都市
ARCHITECTURE AND URBANISM
24:03
642

Feature:
Irish Architecture
20 Houses by 6 Architects

t o b Architect
Killan Farmhouse
Bailieborough, Ireland

This house is in County Cavan, in an area of glacial deposits called drumlins that form a landscape of gentle rolling hills. This landscape produces a rich concentric pattern, with the historical division of land into smallholdings divided by ditches and hedgerows.

Oriented southwest, the house sits on such a hill and is approached by a long passageway that serves the client's farm. It is a 4-bedroom house of conventional rooms, approximately square in plan with these rooms arranged around a central hall. The upper hall is a linear axis through the house from front to back, while a timber portico breaks the square to form a sheltered entrance on the northeast corner.

The house follows the conventional Irish building practice of cavity wall construction. It is rigorous in its adherence to block works capabilities and limits. The setting out of the block work is strict. While the so-called rules of the block work (adherence to its dimensional limits) are reflected in the length and height of the walls and chimney, the form of the roof is determined by the eccentric location of the chimney as the apex of the roof. What I am calling rules, perhaps just prompt judgments. For example, the location of the chimney is a perverse judgment – it operates in the plan by locating the fire hearth, but at roof level it works to deliberately skew the geometry of the roof, making an eccentric pyramidal form.

The indent made in the block-work envelope is a dissolution of the flat massive quality of the block work generally. That mass recedes at the entrance portico and the timber members become free of the wall. Here the timberwork becomes properly structural; it must hold the roof. The timber fins in turn come away from the primary structure, which must now hold both them and the roof.

It appears to us that such judgments are logical.

Credits and Data
Project title: Killan Farmhouse
Client: Private
Location: Bailieborough, county Cavan, Ireland.
Design: 2015
Completion: 2018
Architect: t o b Architect
Design team: Thomas O Brien
Project team: John Murphy (contractor)
Gross floor area: 200 m²

pp. 144–145: Approach to the house. Photos on pp. 144–151 by Aisling McCoy. Opposite: Window detail. This page: Driveway.

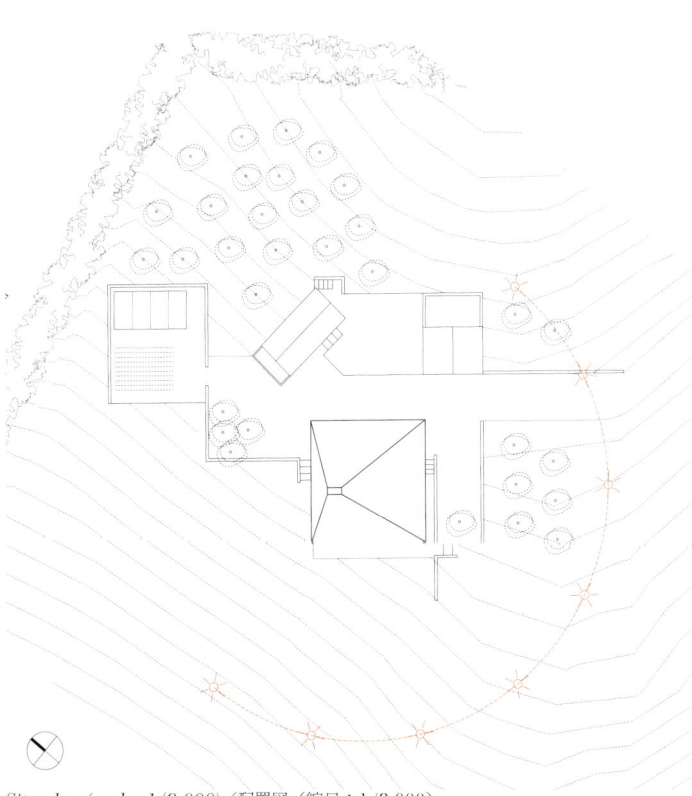

Site plan (scale: 1/8,000)／配置図（縮尺：1/8,000）

p. 148: Kitchen. p. 149: Dining area. This page, top left: 2nd floor corridor. This page, top right: 2nd floor bathroom. This page, bottom left: Staircase leading to the 2nd floor. This page, bottom right: Double height central hall.

148頁:キッチン。149頁:ダイニング・エリア。本頁、左上:2階廊下。本頁、右上:2階浴室。本頁、左下:2階へつづく階段。本頁、右下:吹き抜けの中央ホール。

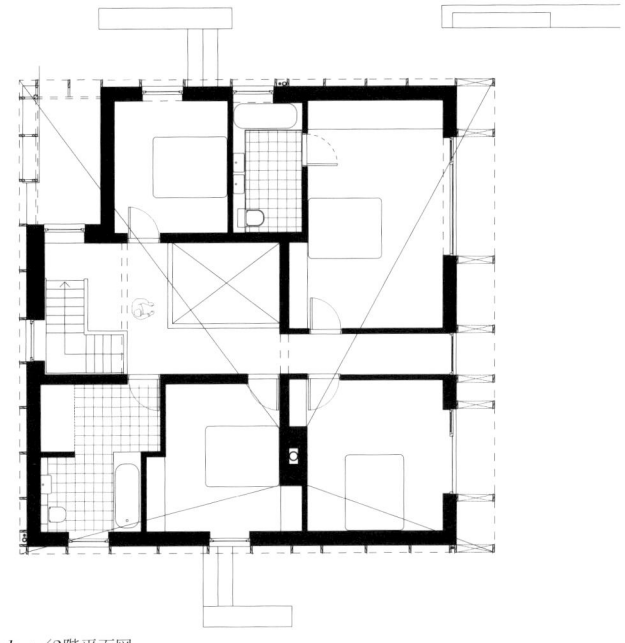

2nd-floor plan／2階平面図

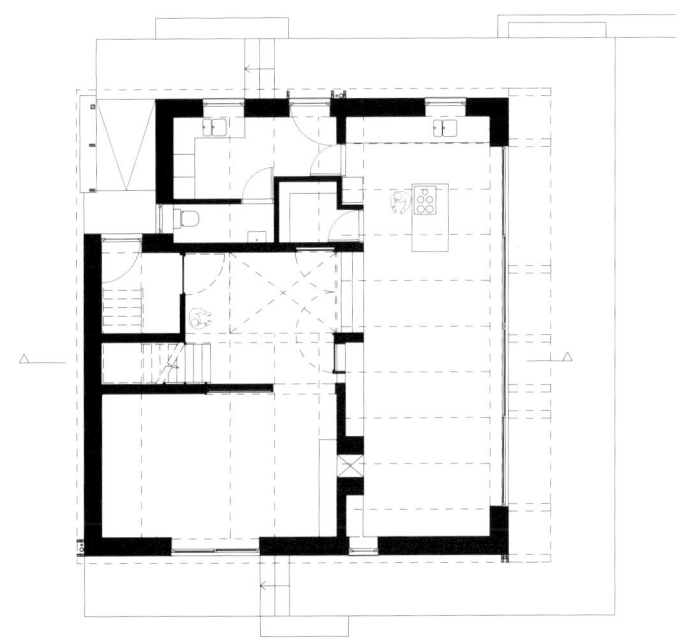

Ground-floor plan (scale: 1/200)／地上階平面図（縮尺：1/200）

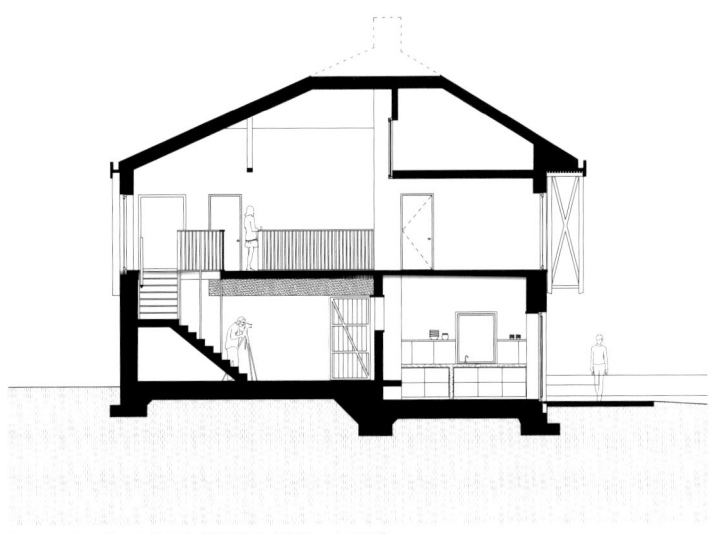

Section (scale: 1/200)／断面図（縮尺：1/200）

t o b Architect
Reuben Street
Dublin, Ireland 2021–2024

t o b アーキテクト
ルーベン・ストリート
アイルランド、ダブリン 2021〜2024

建築と都市
ARCHITECTURE AND URBANISM
24:03

642

Feature:
Irish Architecture
20 Houses by 6 Architects

t o b Architect
Reuben Street
Dublin, Ireland

This is a small project to refurbish and extend a terrace house in Dublin. The addition is a small cubic volume to the rear of the house, to create an additional dining area.

ダブリン市内にあるテラスハウスを改修・増築する小さなプロジェクトである。増築では、住宅の裏手に小さな立方体ヴォリュームを設け、ダイニング・エリアを追加する。

（松本晴子訳）

p. 152: Exterior. Photos on pp. 152–154 by Thomas O Brien. p. 153: Dining area. Opposite: Kitchen.

152頁：外観。153頁：ダイニング・エリア。左頁：キッチン。

Credits and Data
Project title: Reuben Street
Client: Private
Location: Reuben Street, Dublin, Ireland.
Design: 2021
Completion: 2024
Architect: t o b Architect
Design team: Rostyslav Ishchuk (contractor)
Gross floor area: 90 m^2

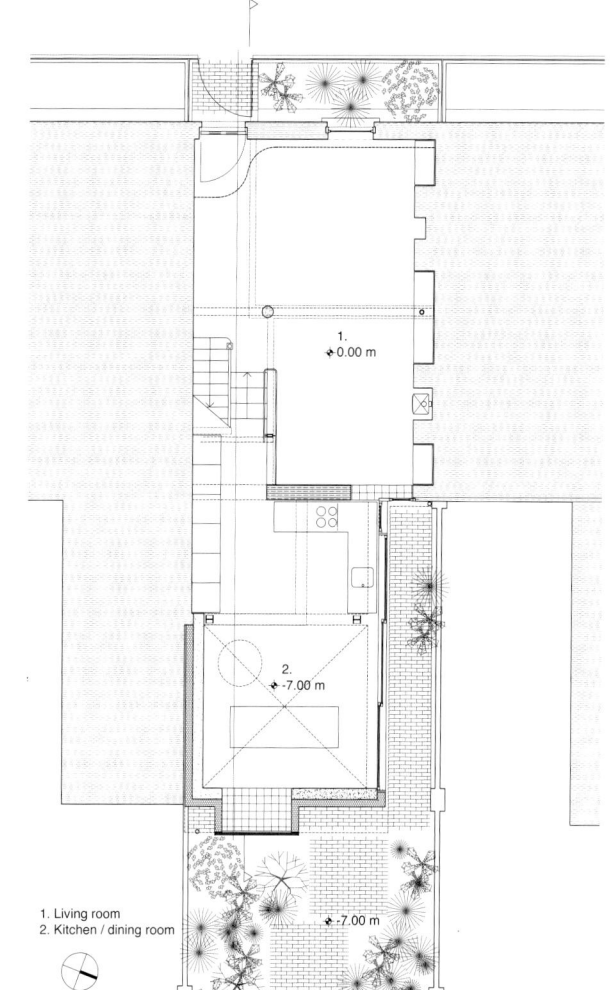

1. Living room
2. Kitchen / dining room

Ground-floor plan (scale: 1/300) ／地上階平面図（縮尺：1/300）

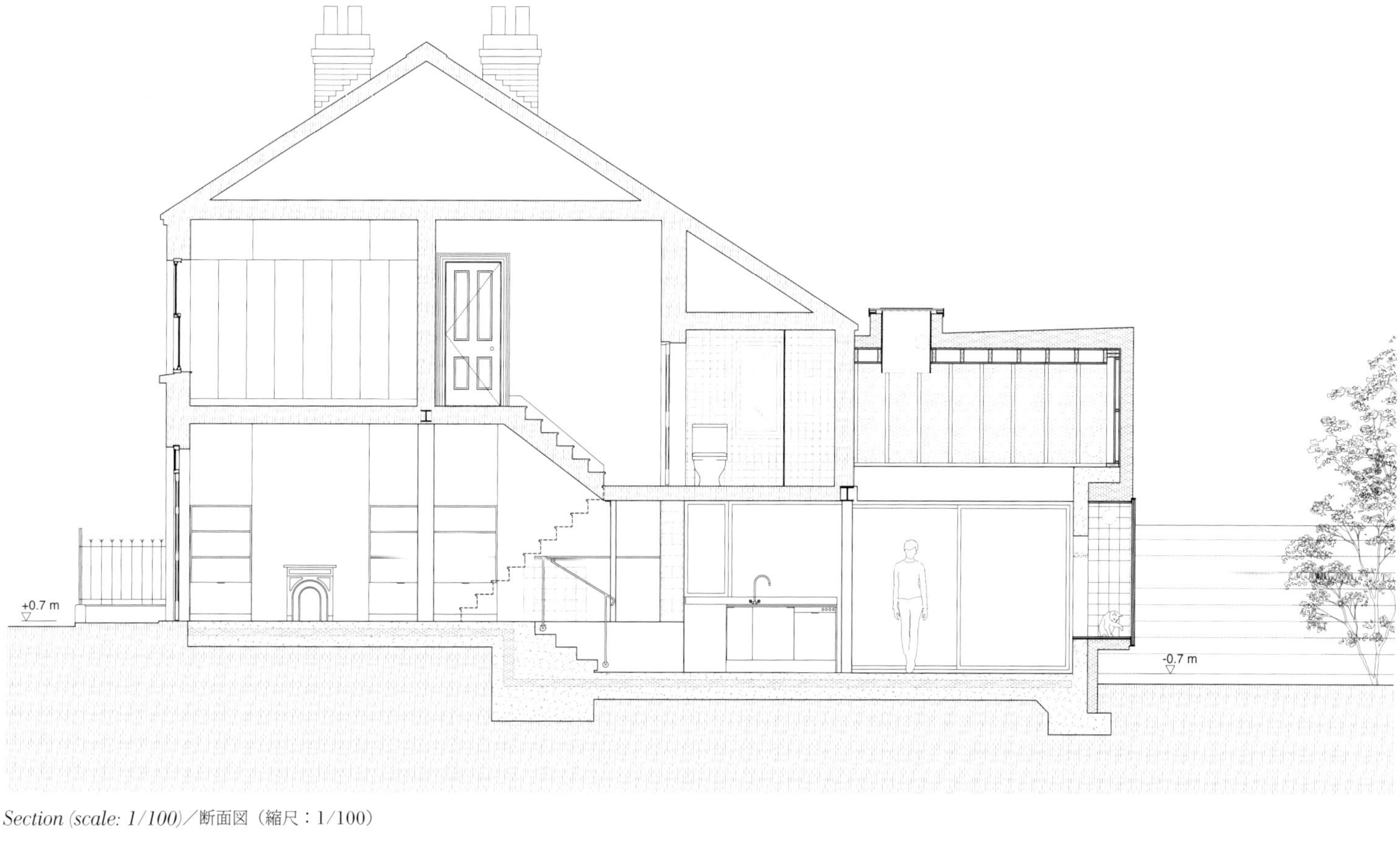

Section (scale: 1/100) ／断面図（縮尺：1/100）

t o b Architect
The Quay
Ramelton, Ireland 2018–2022

t o b アーキテクト
ザ・キー
アイルランド、ラメルトン　2018〜2022

建築と都市 ARCHITECTURE AND URBANISM 24:03

642

Feature:
Irish Architecture
20 Houses by 6 Architects

t o b Architect
The Quay
Ramelton, Ireland

William Stewart, an English mercenary, established the small town of Ramelton between 1609 and 1622, during the Ulster Plantation. In the 18th and 19th centuries, the town prospered as a colonial port with trade extending to Great Britain, North America, Norway, and the Caribbean, and the stone warehouses built around 1830 on the River Lennon quays still reflect that unsettled history. With the coming of the railways in the late 19th century, the prosperity of this small town waned to the nearby town of Letterkenny, and in the 20th century, these buildings came to be known as The Bottling Stores, in reference to their new function as warehousing for a local lemonade manufacturer.

The adaptation and re-use of this historical building was steered by useful constraint, such as the quay's historical and visual status as an iconic piece of town fabric, which meant that the municipality allowed only minimum alterations to its external envelope. These quays tend to flood on an annual basis when spring tides coincide with the increased surge of the river. Within the building, the existing floor-to-ceiling heights were very low at approximately 2 m. Within a modest internal area, the client required 2 dwelling houses, one for himself and one for his children.

These constraints suggested a project of 2 tower houses, dividing the building not in the middle but along the north side of the central opening to conserve the external elevation. A split-level arrangement of rooms around steel stairs draws light all the way down to the ground-floor entrances, while the ground floor is raised 600 mm on a concrete plinth, with the lower entrance area containing no services that might be damaged by water in the eventuality of flooding. While the existing warehouse floorboards were rotten, the original North American pine rafters, joists, and lateral beams were in very good condition. These elements were retained but reconfigured as a permanent shuttering to cast new structural polished concrete floors, which had to align the new stair levels with the existing window locations, while providing adequate floor-to-ceiling heights. Contained by its protected envelope, the emerging project was shaped by constraints, but also our own intent. Its architectural ambition is present in the positioning of things, in the careful judgment of adjacencies.

pp. 156–157: The house seen from across the quay. Photos on pp. 156–165 by Thomas O Brien. Opposite: During renovation.

156〜157頁：波止場の奥に住宅を見る。
右頁：改修の様子。

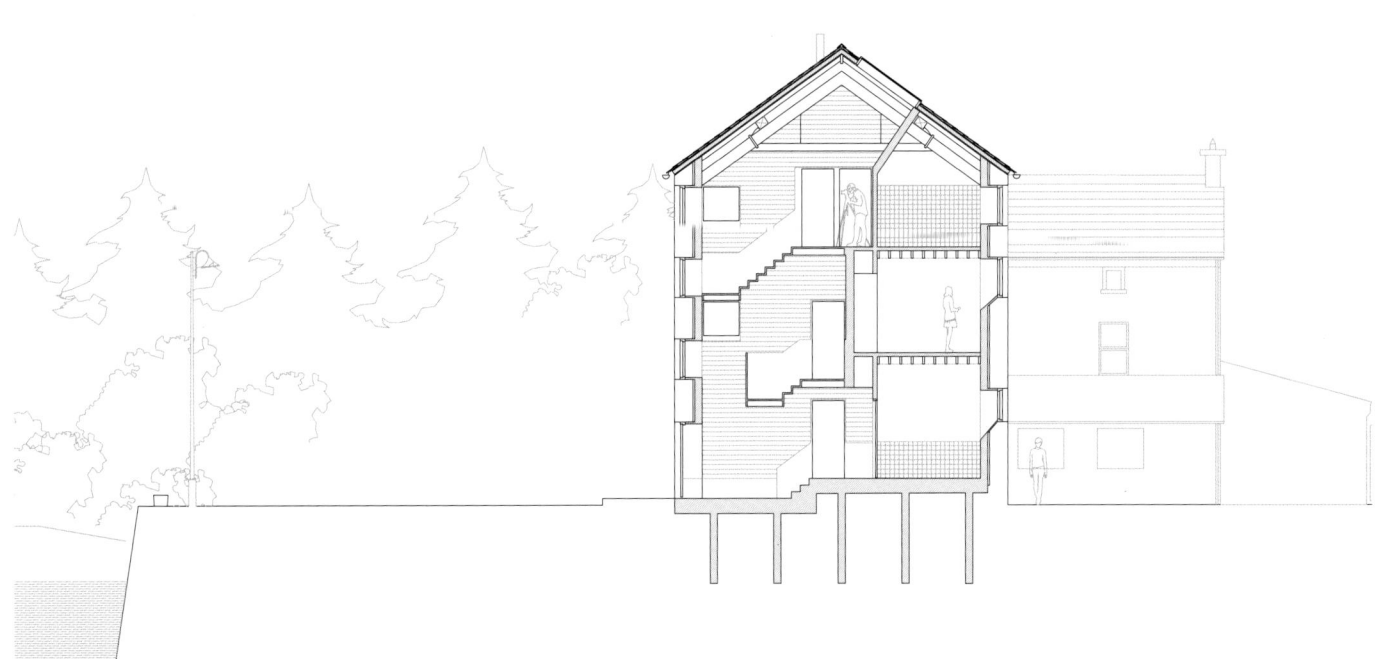

Section (scale: 1/200)／断面図（縮尺：1/200）

3rd-floor plan／3階平面図

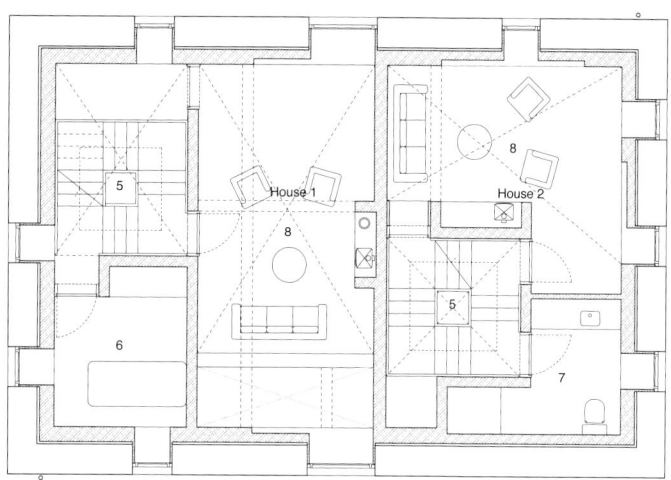

2nd-floor plan／2階平面図

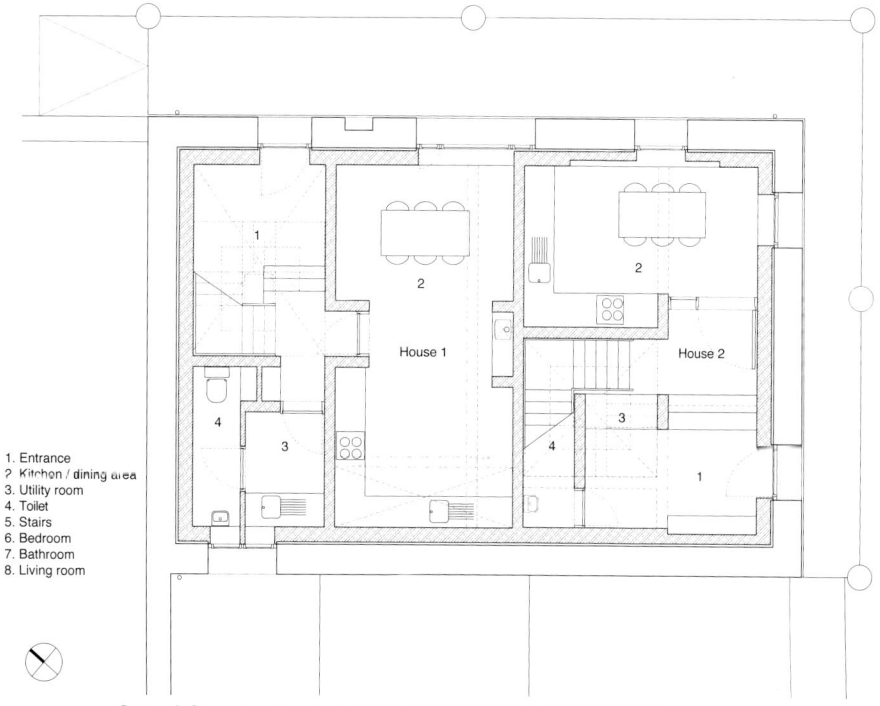

1. Entrance
2. Kitchen / dining area
3. Utility room
4. Toilet
5. Stairs
6. Bedroom
7. Bathroom
8. Living room

Ground-floor plan (scale: 1/150)／地上階平面図（（縮尺：1/150）

161

小さな町ラメルトンは、アルスター植民時代にイギリスの傭兵であるウィリアム・スチュワート卿によって1609年から1622年にかけて設立された。18世紀から19世紀にかけて、植民地港湾都市として栄え、貿易はイギリス、北アメリカ、ノルウェー、カリブ海にまで及び、1830年頃にレノン川岸壁に建てられた石造倉庫群は、その不穏な歴史を今に伝えている。この小さな町の繁栄は、19世紀後半に隣町レタケニーに鉄道が開通したことで衰退した。20世紀にはこれらの建物は、地元のレモネード製造業者の倉庫として新たに機能したことにちなみ、ボトリング・ストアとして知られるようになった。

岸壁は歴史的にも見た目にも町の象徴を担っており、自治体からは外壁の改修を最小限にとどめることが許可された。本改修・再利用プロジェクトはこうした多くの有益な制約によって方向づけられている。大潮と川の増水が重なると、岸壁は毎年洪水に見舞われる。既存の天井高は約2mと非常に低かった。クライアントは、慎ましい内部面積の中に、自分用と子供用、2つの居住スペースを必要としていた。

このような制約から2棟からなる住宅が計画された。建物は中央で分割するのではなく、中央の開口部北側に沿って分割され、外壁の高さを節約できた。鉄骨階段の周りに段差をつけて居室を配置することで、地上階のエントランスまで光を引き込むことが可能となった。地上階はコンクリート台座によって600mm高くなっており、低い箇所にあるエントランス部は万が一洪水が起こった際に水害を受ける可能性があるため、サービス設備は配置していない。既存の床板は腐っていたが、オリジナルのベイマツの垂木、根太、横梁は非常によ状態にあった。これらは残され、既存の窓位置や新しい階段の高さに合わせ、適切な天高を確保するため、磨きコンクリートの構造床を打設するための恒久的なシャッターとして保持・再構成された。

保護された外壁に包まれた新プロジェクトは、制約によってかたちづくられながらも同時に、建築家が意図して行ったことでもある。こうした建築における野心は、物の配置や隣接するものについての慎重な判断の中に存在する。　　　　（松本晴子訳）

p. 160: Stairwell. p. 162–163: Living room of House 1. This page, top: Entrance lobby of House 1. This page, bottom: Hallway. Opposite: Dining area.

160頁：階段。162〜163頁：住宅1の居間。本頁、上：住宅1エントランス・ロビー。本頁、下：廊下。右頁：ダイニング・エリア。

Credits and Data
Project title: The Quay
Client: Private
Location: Ramelton, county Donegal, Ireland
Design: 2018
Completion: 2022
Architect: t o b Architect
Design team: Thomas O Brien
Project team: Daniel McGrory (contractor)
Gross floor area: 200 m²

Profiles

プロフィール

Andrew Clancy and Colm Moore founded **Clancy Moore Architects** in 2008 and have gained an international reputation for projects including cultural, infrastructural, and residential works. The practice frequently works with complex or sensitive sites, such as that for the Arklow Wastewater project, and has an expertise in collaboratively engaging with a vast array of external specialisms depending on the context. Both partners research and seek to advance architecture through critical enquiry and academic works. Both have PhDs in practice from RMIT University. Clancy is professor of architecture in Kingston School of Art, while Moore directs the MArch at Queen's University Belfast. Both are guest professors at the Academy of Architecture of Mendrisio – directing a research and design atelier that investigates fictions and situated understandings as sites for architectural production.
Their book about the Danish architect Kay Fisker was published in 2022, and a survey of their work will issue in 2024 in *De aedibus* series from Quart Verlag.

アンドリュー・クランシーとコルム・ムーアは2008年に**クランシー・ムーア・アーキテクツ**を設立し、文化施設・インフラ・住宅などのプロジェクトで国際的評価を得る。アークロウ廃水プロジェクトのような複雑でデリケートな敷地を扱うことも多く、コンテクストに応じて外部専門家の協力を得ることに長けている。両パートナーは、批評的探求や学術を通して建築を研究進歩させようとしている。両者ともRMIT大学で博士号を取得。クランシーはキングストン美術学校で建築学教授を務め、ムーアはクイーンズ大学ベルファスト校でMArchを指導。両者ともメンドリジオ建築アカデミーの客員教授であり、建築制作の場としての虚構や状況理解を調査する研究・設計アトリエを指導している。
デンマークの建築家ケイ・フィスカーに関する著書が2022年にLund Humphries社から出版され、2024年にはQuart Verlag社の『De aedibus』シリーズで彼らの作品が特集される予定。

Steve Larkin Architects is an architectural practice based in Dublin, Ireland. They are focused on designing and making carefully crafted buildings that are sensitive to their physical and cultural context. They have a wide range of project types ranging from domestic to commercial and public works.
They emphasize the importance of object, detail, and space to produce carefully honed architecture. They take a careful, practical, and economic approach to materials and construction. Sustainability is considered from first principle at all stages of the design process. They collaborate closely with clients, professional consultants, and expert tradespeople to ensure that project ambitions are met. Steve Larkin Architects's international exhibition commissions include the 16th Venice Biennale of Architecture and the London Festival of Architecture 2015. The work of the practice has been exhibited and published worldwide. Research outputs include buildings, exhibitions, symposiums, conferences, and publications.

スティーブ・ラーキン・アーキテクツはアイルランドのダブリンを拠点とする建築事務所。物理・文化的コンテクストに配慮した建築物の設計施工に力を注ぐ。住宅から商業施設や公共施設まで、プロジェクトは多岐にわたる。
注意深く研ぎ澄まされた建築を生みだすため、オブジェ・ディテール・空間を重要視する。素材や構造には慎重かつ実用・経済的アプローチをとる。設計プロセスの全段階において、サステナビリティを第一義的に考慮する。クライアント、専門コンサルタント、専門業者と密に協力し、プロジェクトの目標を達成する。
スティーブ・ラーキン・アーキテクツは、第16回ヴェネチア建築ビエンナーレやロンドン・フェスティバル・オブ・アーキテクチュア2015など、国際的展覧会に出展。作品は世界中で展示、出版されている。研究成果には、建築物、展覧会、シンポジウム、会議、出版物などがある。